Emotion

THE SCIENCE OF SENTIMENT

Dylan Evans

OXFORD
UNIVERSITY PRESS

OXFORD

UNIVERSITY PRESS

Great Clarendon Street, Oxford OX2 6DP

Oxford University Press is a department of the University of Oxford.
It furthers the University's objective of excellence in research, scholarship,
and education by publishing worldwide in

Oxford New York

Athens Auckland Bangkok Bogotá Buenos Aires Calcutta
Cape Town Chennai Dar es Salaam Delhi Florence Hong Kong Istanbul
Karachi Kuala Lumpur Madrid Melbourne Mexico City Mumbai
Nairobi Paris São Paulo Shanghai Singapore Taipei Tokyo Toronto Warsaw

with associated companies in Berlin Ibadan

Oxford is a registered trade mark of Oxford University Press
in the UK and in certain other countries

Published in the United States
by Oxford University Press Inc., New York

British Library Cataloguing in Publication Data

Data available

Library of Congress Cataloging in Publication Data

Data available

ISBN 0–19–285433–X

1 3 5 7 9 10 8 6 4 2

Typeset in New Baskerville
by RefineCatch Limited, Bungay, Suffolk
Printed in Spain by Book Print S. L.

To Em, my Tygress, my one and only true love

Acknowledgements

Thanks are due to my editor at Oxford University Press, Shelley Cox, and my agent, Louise Greenberg, for their publishing expertise. Shelley and Louise also read various versions of the book and gave me useful suggestions for improvement. Four anonymous readers commissioned by Oxford University Press made helpful suggestions at the proposal stage.

The following people shared ideas and gave me useful feedback on various things I have written about emotion in the past few years: Rosalind Arden, Helena Cronin, Oliver Curry, Paul Ekman, Paul Griffiths, Nicholas Humphrey, Geoffrey Miller, Randolph Nesse, Keith Oatley, David Papineau, Robert Plomin, Dan Sperber, Lewis Wolpert, John Worrall, and all the people at the Darwin@LSE Work-in-Progress group. Paul Hilder checked the entire book with his usual eagle-eyed attention to detail. James Ottaway provided some useful references on the effects of winning the lottery. Anna Maconochie told me the story of Johnny Ace, and Tom Polseno gave me the idea of using Commander Data to illustrate moral law theory. My mother, Jeannie Benjamin, rooted out some nice quotations for me to use, and my father Ken Evans sent me a useful anthology of essays. Thanks to Chris Redston for sharing his views on happiness, and to my sister Charlotte for her unstinting support.

Finally, thanks to Em, whose nobility of sentiment has restored my faith in the human capacity for transcendence.

Contents

Preface

The word 'sentiment' has fallen on hard times. Today, it is hardly used, and its cousin, 'sentimental', has negative connotations. Two and a half centuries ago, towards the end of the Enlightenment, things were very different. Then, sentiment meant roughly what 'emotion' means today.

The philosophers of the Enlightenment were fascinated by the emotions. David Hume, Adam Smith, and Thomas Reid all wrote at length about the sentiments and the passions. These thinkers believed that emotions were vital to individual and social existence. Smith did not just found the 'dismal science' (economics); he also helped to pioneer the 'sentimental science' (the psychology of emotion). In his first book, *The Theory of Moral Sentiments* (1759), he proposed that emotions were the thread that wove together the fabric of society. Like Hume and Reid, Smith did not regard emotion and thought as implacable enemies. For all of these thinkers, it was rational to be emotional, and no science of the mind could be complete without also addressing the heart.

The Romantics rejected this view, reviving an older

view of emotions as fundamentally at odds with reason. Humans were faced with a stark choice between emotion and reason, and the wise ones chose to follow their hearts rather than their heads. Rousseau argued that reason had led man out of his innocent 'state of nature' into decadence. To return to innocence meant listening to one's feelings rather than consulting logic. The secrets of sentiment were to be unlocked by poetry, not by science.

I have used the word 'sentiment' in the subtitle of this book to signal my sympathy with the Enlightenment view of emotion. Unlike the Romantics, I do not believe that emotions are fundamentally at odds with reason, nor that we should always follow our hearts rather than our heads. Rather, like Adam Smith, I believe that intelligent action results from a harmonious blend of emotion and reason. I believe that a creature without emotions would be less rational than us, not more, but I also believe that there are times when it is better to listen to the head rather than the heart. Knowing when to follow our feelings and when to ignore them is a valuable talent that some have called 'emotional intelligence'.

In this book I argue for a return to the view of emotions as reason's ally, not its enemy. Like Smith and Hume, I believe that the scientific study of emotion is not only possible, but of great value. This is not because I think we can ever reduce emotional experience to a dry formula. However, thinking more clearly about emotion need not be opposed to feeling more deeply. It is my hope that knowing more about how emotions work can help us to lead richer lives, not poorer. At the very least, it can be exciting to learn about the recent scientific advances in our understanding of these mysterious phenomena.

Scientific interest in the emotions underwent something of a renaissance in the 1990s. For much of the twentieth century, research in the emotions was confined to a few psychologists and even fewer anthropologists. At the dawn of the twenty-first century, however, things are rather different. Emotion is now a hot topic. Anthropologists have begun to question their previous views on the cultural relativity of emotional experience. Cognitive psychologists have abandoned their exclusive focus on reasoning, perception, and memory, and are rediscovering the importance of affective processes. Neuroscientists and researchers in artificial intelligence have also joined the debate, contributing further pieces to the jigsaw. This book attempts to step back and put some of these pieces together.

Needless to say, a short book like this cannot hope to cover all aspects of such a complex area. I have had to leave some very interesting areas of emotion research to one side. The reader will not find, for example, a discussion of how emotions develop in children, although this too is a burgeoning area of study. Nor is there any mention of the growing literature on individual differences in emotional experience. My choice of topics reflects my own idiosyncratic interests and my guesses about what will prove most interesting to you.

I start with a discussion of the variety of emotional experiences in different cultures. Every culture has its own emotional climate, and I draw on anthropological research that has documented some of these variations. However, many anthropologists now think that the differences between emotional experiences around the world are minor when compared with the similarities. In Chapter One I argue that emotions constitute a kind of 'universal language' that binds humanity together into a single family. Our common emotional heritage goes deeper than the cultural differences that set us apart.

We owe this shared emotional repertoire to our common ancestry. We are all descended from a few thousand hominids who lived on the African plains a hundred thousand years ago. Many of our emotions were forged in this bygone age. Many more emotions go back even further, to a time when our ancestors were not even human. In Chapter Two I explore the evolutionary history of emotion, and argue that emotions were—and still are—vital for survival. Emotions are not just luxuries. Still less are they obstacles to intelligent action, as Plato believed. The creators of *Star Trek* were wrong to suppose that the Vulcans, an imaginary alien race that lacked emotions, would be more intelligent than humans. Spock notwithstanding, an intelligent creature that lacked emotions simply could not evolve.

Of course, we now live in very different environments from those in which our ancestors evolved. In particular, we have many means of inducing happiness in ourselves that our ancestors never even dreamt of. In Chapter Three I discuss these 'technologies of mood' that promise to provide us with short cuts to happiness, from psychotherapy and art to drugs and meditation. I ask whether or not they work, and discuss the dangers that beset some of these attempts to circumvent the more circuitous path to happiness that natural selection laid out for us.

In Chapter Four I explain how emotions affect 'cognitive' capacities such as memory, attention, and perception. The power of emotions to affect these things makes emotional technologies very appealing to advertisers and politicians. Appealing to feelings offers a way of making people change their minds without having to provide good arguments or evidence. I conclude the chapter with a discussion of the various emotional technologies of persuasion such as subliminal advertising.

The most recent discipline to have entered the debate on emotion is artificial intelligence. Since the early 1990s, computer scientists have become increasingly interested in building emotional machines, and workers in robotics are already making some progress in this area. In the final chapter I discuss these recent developments, and speculate on where it will all lead. Will we succeed in building robots that have feelings just like we do? And what might be the consequences of such technology?

I do not pretend to have the last word on emotion. A really good theory of emotion may remain forever beyond our grasp. However, I find the attempt to construct such a theory a fascinating thing in its own right. I hope that reading this book will lead you to share my enthusiasm.

Dylan Evans

London
September 2000

1

The universal language

When I was 15, some friends of mine invited me to join their punk rock band. The previous singer, while very good in rehearsals, suffered from stage fright, and could not perform in public. I was just the opposite: my voice was terrible, but I had no qualms about making a fool of myself. Just the right ingredients for a punk rock singer!

After the first rehearsal, we sat around planning our careers in the music business. It was then that Tim told me how happy he was that I had joined the band. I can still remember vividly the intense reaction that comment produced in me. A warm wave spread outwards and upwards from my stomach, rapidly enveloping the whole of my upper chest. It was a kind of joy, but unlike any moment of joy I had felt before. It was a feeling of acceptance, of belonging, of being valued by a group of people whom I was proud to call my friends. I was momentarily lost for words, shocked by the novelty of the sensation. In the years since then, the feeling has never repeated itself exactly, and I have never forgotten it.

I am certainly not the only person to have experienced this particular emotion. Millions of football fans and religious worshippers seem to feel something similar every weekend. And yet there is no word for it in English. Just now, when I was describing it, I had to use several words: 'a kind of joy, a feeling of acceptance, of belonging, of being valued by a group of people . . .'. Perhaps the closest thing to a name for this emotion is a phrase that was coined by Romain Rolland: the 'oceanic feeling'. But even this poetic expression requires two words. Would it not be easier if we just had one?

In Japan, it seems, they do. The word *amae* means just the kind of 'comfort in another person's complete acceptance' that I felt when Tim made his comment. The original Chinese ideogram was of a breast on which the baby suckled, which suggests that this emotion involves a loss of separateness, a return to the sense of oneness that fuses mother and child together in the first months of life.

Why is there no word for *amae* in English? The different ways in which various languages carve up the world reflect different cultural needs. Perhaps the Japanese need a word for *amae* because the emotion it designates accords with the fundamental values of Japanese culture. Unlike the situation in the English-speaking world, which prizes independence, self-assertion, and autonomy, in Japan it is often more important to fit in with others and live in harmonious groups. *Amae* is an emotion that helps people to comply with these values.

Whatever the reason for this particular difference between the English and Japanese *languages*, it does not point to any fundamental difference between the *people* of England and Japan. As an English speaker, I do not have a precise term to describe the emotion I felt at Tim's house, but that did not stop me from *feeling* that emotion. On the contrary; the emotion just happened, without warning, and left me groping for words to describe it. Years later, when I read a description of *amae*, I knew immediately that it named the emotion I had felt that evening at Tim's house. People all over the world experience this emotion, but only some of them have a word for it.

The cultural theory of emotion

All this seems quite straightforward. Yet, for a large part of the twentieth century, many anthropologists would have turned their noses up at the last paragraph, for they subscribed to a view known as the cultural theory of emotion. According to this view, emotions are learned behaviours, transmitted culturally, much like languages. Just as you must first hear English before you can speak it, so you must first see others being joyful before you can feel joy. You could certainly not feel *amae* unless you had been brought up in a culture in which *amae* was commonly expressed and discussed. On this theory, people living in different cultures should experience different emotions.

In the late 1960s, while this view of emotion was still the reigning orthodoxy, a young American anthropologist called Paul Ekman set out to find firm scientific evidence in its favour. To his great surprise, he ended up doing just the opposite. Ekman's studies provided the first scientific evidence that the cultural theory of emotion was badly off the mark.

Ekman's methodology was simple but clever. He travelled to a remote, preliterate culture (the Fore, in New Guinea) to ensure that the subjects had not seen Western photographs or films, and so could never have *learned* Western emotions. Ekman then told them various stories, and asked them to choose, from three photographs of Americans expressing various emotions, the photo that most closely matched the story.

For example, one story involved coming across a wild

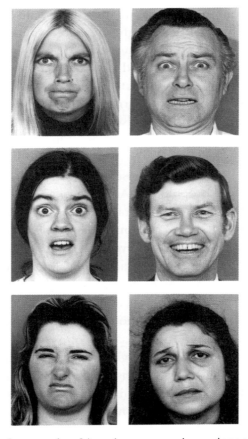

1 Some photographs of Americans expressing various emotions. Paul Ekman used these photographs in his cross-cultural research.

pig when alone in a hut, a situation that would elicit fear in Westerners. Sure enough, the Fore pointed to the same expressions that Westerners linked to the stories. Just to be sure, Ekman asked some Fore people to make facial expressions appropriate to each of the stories and videotaped them. On returning to San Francisco, he did the experiment in reverse, asking Americans to link the Fore faces to the stories. Once again, the judgements tallied.

When Ekman first presented his results to the American Anthropological Association, he was met with cries of derision. The cultural theory of emotion was so entrenched that any criticisms were simply laughed out of court. Eventually, however, Ekman won the argument. It is now widely accepted among emotion researchers that some emotions, at least, are not learned. They are universal, and innate.

Ekman called these emotions 'basic'. Researchers disagree about how many basic emotions there are, but there is a consensus emerging that they include joy, distress, anger, fear, surprise, and disgust (see Box below). There is no culture in which these emotions are absent. Moreover, they are not learned; they are hard-wired into the human brain. This much is clear from the fact that babies who are born blind still make the facial expressions typical of these emotions—smiling,

Basic emotions

Basic emotions are universal and innate. They are of rapid onset and last a few seconds at a time. Researchers disagree about how many basic emotions there are, but most would include the following in their list:

- Joy
- Distress
- Anger
- Fear
- Surprise
- Disgust

Some researchers call these emotions by different names. It is common, for example, to see 'happiness' and 'sadness' in the list of basic emotions. I think these words are better used to describe moods rather than emotions (see Chapter Three), so in this book I use the words 'joy' and 'distress' to refer to basic emotions and reserve the terms 'happiness' and 'sadness' for good and bad moods.

grimacing, and so on. Emotional expressions are not like words, which differ from culture to culture; they are closer to breathing, which is just part of human nature.

Of course, the diehard proponent of the cultural

2 In these two self-portrait etchings, Rembrandt shows the facial expressions of two basic emotions: surprise and anger.

theory of emotion can always retort that Ekman's studies showed only that the *facial expressions* associated with basic emotions are universal and innate. The studies tell us nothing about the subjective feelings behind those expressions. This is true enough, but the same applies to *everything* that is private and subjective. I can never be sure, for example, that your experience of the colour red, or your sense of the sweetness of sugar, are the same as mine. However, if our subjective experiences were really so radically different, it is difficult to know how we could ever communicate at all. We might be able to use the same words in a similarly grammatical fashion, but, if we were using them to represent fundamentally different concepts, we would surely end up in a hopeless muddle of misunderstandings. We would never be able to agree about anything.

Now, while disagreement and misunderstanding are certainly common, they are not so common as to prevent all effective communication. Most of us seem to get our message across most of the time. When I first read the description of *amae* in a book about emotions, I knew immediately what it meant, even though there is no simple translation for it in English. Likewise, when we read poems and novels written by authors from other cultures, we recognize the emotions they describe. If emotions were cultural inventions, changing as swiftly as language, these texts would seem alien and impenetrable.

Communication is possible without words too. And this is largely thanks to the basic emotions we all share. When anthropologists first come into contact with a previously isolated people, their only means of communication is via facial expressions and bodily gestures, many of which are specifically designed to express emotions. The anthropologists may smile, an expression that will be recognized immediately by the isolated tribespeople. The tribespeople may smile in return, showing the anthropologists that they share the same feeling.

Our common emotional heritage binds humanity together, then, in a way that transcends cultural difference. In all places, and at all times, human beings have shared the same basic emotional repertoire. Different cultures have elaborated on this repertoire, exalting different emotions, downgrading others, and embellishing the common feelings with cultural nuances, but these differences are more like those between two interpretations of the same musical work, rather than those between different compositions. Just as two orchestras will play the same symphony slightly differently, so two cultures will play out their emotional

3 The facial expressions for basic emotions are the same all over the world.

repertoire in different tones. It will be clear to all, however, that the score is the same.

The universality of basic emotions argues strongly for their biological nature. If basic emotions were cultural inventions, their ubiquity would be very surprising indeed. If we suppose, however, that they are part of humanity's common biological inheritance, then their presence throughout the world is easy to explain. Just as all human beings have the same kind of body, with minor variations, so we all have the same kind of mind. This universal human nature is encoded in the human genome, the legacy of our shared evolutionary history.

Today, there are over six billion human beings, and they are spread out all over the globe. A hundred thousand years ago, however, there were only a few thousand human beings on the planet, and they all lived in a small region of East Africa. All the human beings alive today are descended from this small population, some of whom left Africa at some point and began the slow business of colonizing the rest of the world.

When they left Africa, our ancestors all looked the same. They all had black skin, for example. Then, as different human groups moved into new areas, they evolved in slightly different ways. Skin colour is the most obvious of these differences. The differences, however, are literally just skin-deep. Our internal organs, including our brains, are basically the same the world over. Since basic emotions are largely determined by the structure of our brains, it really should come as no surprise that they too are fundamentally the same in all cultures.

Now that the psychological unity of humankind is more widely acknowledged, it can be hard to understand how the cultural theory of emotion ever gained such widespread acceptance. Perhaps the answer lies in the (equally universal) human tendency to exaggerate the small differences between the various human groups. In the search for cultural identity, we naturally fix on the things that set us apart from others, rather than on the things that link us together. When it comes to emotions, we often pay attention to the small cultural differences, and ignore the overwhelming similarities.

European attitudes to the peoples of South-East Asia are a case in point. For a long time in England and other parts of Europe, people from Japan, China, and countries in South-East Asia were commonly described as being mysterious and unfathomable. This stereotype of the 'inscrutable oriental' was due in large part to the fact that European travellers found it hard to read their emotions. They wondered whether the poker face of the Japanese might conceal emotions that were very different from their own.

The Japanese do, in fact, take greater pains to hide their emotions than do people in Europe and North America. Every culture has its own rules that define the socially acceptable forms of emotional expression. In Europe and North America, these 'display rules' encourage vivid facial expressions of emotion; a poker face is generally regarded as dull or deceptive. In Japan, on the other hand, excessive emotional displays are often perceived as rude, and Japanese people consequently make more of an effort to attenuate their emotional expressions.

Underneath these display rules, however, the emotions are the same. In an interesting experiment conducted by Paul Ekman and Wallace Friesen, American and Japanese men were videotaped while they watched film clips. Some of the clips were of neutral or pleasant events, such as a canoe trip, while others were of rather disgusting things such as a ritual circumcision, the suction-aided delivery of a baby, and nasal surgery. In one showing, the subjects watched the clips in private, while in another an interviewer was present. When alone, similar facial expressions were observed in both American and Japanese subjects. When the interviewer was present, however, the Japanese smiled more and showed less disgust than their American counterparts.

The most interesting thing about this experiment,

however, became apparent only when the videotapes were viewed in slow motion. Only then was it possible to observe that, when the interviewer was present, the Japanese subjects actually started to make the same expressions of disgust as the Americans did, and succeeded in masking these expressions only a few fractions of a second later. In other words, the same basic emotions were felt by both the Americans and the Japanese. These biological responses were automatic, beyond voluntary control. Only after consciousness caught up, a few hundred milliseconds later, could the learned display rules be imposed on top of the basic biological response.

The inscrutable oriental, then, is concealing not radically different emotions, but the very same emotions as those felt by all other human beings the world over. The European travellers who suspected that an alien mind lurked beneath the less expressive oriental countenance were misled by the superficial differences between their display rules.

As the experiment with the American and Japanese men demonstrates, basic emotions such as fear and disgust are automatic, reflex-like responses over which we have little conscious control. And, like reflexes, they are much faster than anything we do voluntarily. Thus the culturally determined display rules always arrive on the scene after the basic emotional response has been set in motion. The basic emotions are hardwired, etched into our neural circuitry by our genes rather than by our culture, part of the basic mental design that is common to us all.

On being a wild pig

The same is not true for all emotions, however. Some emotions, it seems, really *are* culturally specific. There is an emotion felt by the Gururumba people of New Guinea, for example, that is apparently never experienced by people from other cultures. It is known as the state of 'being a wild pig', because people who experience it behave just like wild pigs: they run wild, looting articles of small value and attacking bystanders.

Emotions like this would certainly not qualify as 'basic' in Ekman's sense of the word. They are not universal. Nor are they innate. Now, the word 'innate' has been used in lots of quite different ways, and some biologists and philosophers have recently argued that we should abandon the term altogether. I think the term is fine, so long as we are careful to say what we mean by it. When I say that some trait is 'innate', I mean that it needs very few special conditions for it to develop. In other words, so long as you give a child the basic things it needs to survive, such as food, shelter, and company, that child will develop all the traits that are innate in humans. Language is innate in this sense; you do not need to provide lots of special instruction materials for a child to acquire a language. All you need to do is bring the child up in a group of other humans who can speak. The ability to speak a particular language, such as English or Japanese, is, of course, not innate. Special conditions over and above the basic necessities for survival are required for such a trait to develop. These conditions do not obtain everywhere.

In saying, then, that culturally specific emotions are not innate, all I am saying is that they will not develop unless special conditions are in place, conditions that are provided only by particular cultures. The main such condition is that you *learn* about this emotion when you are a child. In other words, unlike basic emotions, which develop willy-nilly, culturally specific emotions develop only if you are exposed to them by your culture. For emotions like 'being a wild pig', then, it really *is* the case that you would not feel them unless you had first heard about them. It is this that distinguishes them from basic emotions such as fear or anger, which you would have the capacity to feel even if you had never heard of them.

The fact that different cultures can produce human

beings with different emotional repertoires is testimony to the remarkable plasticity of the human mind. If you believe that the human mind works in a particular way, then, even if your theory is wildly inaccurate as an account of human psychology in general, *your* mind will probably start behaving partly as your theory predicts. In other words, theories about the mind are, to some extent, self-fulfilling prophecies. If your culture teaches you that there is an emotion called 'being a wild pig', then the chances are that you will experience this emotion. And this experience will not be a calculated act of deception. If deception is involved at all, it is a kind of *self*-deception, though this is probably not a very good way of putting things, as culturally specific emotions do not *feel* fake. In fact, they feel no different from basic emotions, which are universal and innate. Gururumba men (it is only men who experience this emotion) really feel as if the emotion of 'being a wild pig' has taken them over against their will, in the same way that basic emotions such as fear or disgust just 'happen to us', without any conscious decision on our part. Those in the grip of culturally specific emotions like 'being a wild pig' are not faking it.

An interesting feature of culturally specific emotions like 'being a wild pig' is that they often provide people with a way out of difficult situations. Gururumba men who are in the grip of this emotion are treated with remarkable tolerance; the emotion is seen as an unwelcome but involuntary event, and so people suffering from it are given special consideration, which includes temporary relief from their financial obligations. By a curious coincidence, it so happens that the emotion is mainly experienced by men aged between 25 and 35—precisely the age when they first encounter the financial difficulties that arise in the early years of marriage. How fortunate it is that, just when a man's economic obligations increase, he may experience an emotion that causes others to allow him some leeway in meeting those obligations.

Of course, it is really no coincidence that the state of 'being a wild pig' afflicts just those people who might derive some benefit from it. The psychologist James Averill has argued that it is precisely the function of many emotions that they help people to cope with the particular demands of their culture. If this is true, it is true only of culturally specific emotions. Basic emotions are not tailored to fit the specific demands of a particular culture, but designed to help us meet the fundamental challenges faced by humans everywhere, as we will see in the next chapter.

Enduring love?

From the way I have presented things so far, it might seem as if there were two quite clear-cut categories of emotion. On the one hand, there are basic emotions, which are universal and innate. On the other hand, there are culturally specific emotions such as 'being a wild pig'. However, things are not really this simple. Innateness is not an all-or-nothing thing, but a question of degree. When investigating emotions or any other biological or psychological trait, we should not really ask whether it is innate or not, but rather *how* innate it is. The more 'special conditions' over and above the basic necessities of survival that are required for the development of a trait, the less innate it is. Learning a language is less innate than growing legs, since growing legs requires only a normal genome, basic nutrition, and the luck to escape nasty accidents, whereas learning a language requires all these things *plus* interaction with other speaking humans. Learning English is less innate still, since it requires that the other speaking humans be English-speakers.

So, rather than thinking of basic and culturally spe-cific emotions as two completely different kinds of thing, we should see them as sitting at opposite ends of a single spectrum. Depending on how many special conditions are required for a given emotion to develop, and on how special they are, the emotion will be located more towards the 'basic' end of the spectrum or more towards the 'culturally specific' end. Basic emotions are much more innate than culturally specific emotions, but they still require some minimal conditions to develop.

With some emotions, it is relatively easy to see where they are located on the innateness spectrum. There is much evidence to suggest that fear and anger are very basic, while it is clear that 'being a wild pig' is very culture specific. With other emotions, however, things are not so clear. One emotion in particular that has divided opinion is romantic love. Some maintain that it is a universal emotion, hardwired into the brain just like fear and anger. Others disagree, arguing that romantic love is more like the state of 'being a wild pig'. La Rochefoucauld famously declared that 'some people would never have fallen in love if they had never heard of love'. Those who think romantic love is a culturally specific emotion go even further: they claim that *nobody* would fall in love if they had not previously heard romantic stories.

The most famous proponent of this view was the writer C. S. Lewis, who argued that romantic love was invented in Europe in the early twelfth century. It was around this time that 'courtly love' became the central theme of much European poetry. In many of the poems a nobleman would fall in love with a lady at the royal court. He would become her knight and devote himself to her service, though his passion for her would rarely be consummated. The love of Lancelot for King Arthur's wife, Guinevere, is perhaps the best-known story to emerge from this literary genre.

If romantic love really *were* an invention of some medieval poets, nobody could have felt this emotion before the Middle Ages. C. S. Lewis was quite happy to accept this consequence of his provocative thesis, and proclaimed that 'no one falls in love in Homer or Virgil'.

This must surely be among the front-running candidates for the most ridiculous idea of the twentieth century. It seems hard to believe that a sensitive man like C. S. Lewis could fail to detect the unmistakable passion expressed in the *Song of Songs*, a book in the Old Testament:

> What a wound thou hast made, my bride, my true love.
> What a wound thou hast made in this heart of mine!
> And all with one glance of an eye,
> All with one ringlet straying on thy neck!

Yet this text pre-dates the medieval poetry of courtly

4 Romantic love: is it just a literary invention?

love by over a thousand years. In fact, romantic love probably goes back much further than this, perhaps even to the dawn of humankind. A hundred thousand years ago, while our ancestors were still confined to the African plains, their physical activities were very different from ours, but their emotional lives were probably very similar. The first humans spent much of their time scouring the terrain for edible plants and making temporary shelters, activities now completely absent from all but a few human communities. But many evolutionary psychologists have argued that they also spent a lot of time getting infatuated with one another, making love, feeling jealous, and getting heartbroken, just as we do today.

Romantic love can also be found in cultures separated from our own by space as well as time, in the remote preliterate societies studied by anthropologists. Yet, if romantic love were a European invention, it could not be experienced by peoples who had had no contact with Europe. This simple consideration allowed two anthropologists to put the cultural theory of romantic love to the test. First, they needed a working definition of romantic love, so they identified the following core features of the idea: a powerful feeling of sexual attraction to a single person, feelings of anguish and longing when the loved one is absent, and intense joy when he or she is present. They also listed other elements, including elaborate courtship gestures such as giving gifts and showing one's love in song and poetry. They then examined the anthropological literature and counted the number of cultures in which this collection of features was described. To their surprise, they found that it was described in 90 per cent of the cultures on record. If anthropologists have actually *observed and noted down* incidents of romantic love in 90 per cent of the societies they have studied, it is a fair bet that this emotion exists in the remaining 10 per cent too.

In the light of all this evidence, it seems hard to believe that anyone could doubt the universality of romantic love. However, there is a small grain of truth in the view of romantic love as a European invention. Even basic emotions differ from culture to culture, though only to a small degree. To return to the musical analogy, the symphony sounds slightly different when played by different orchestras, even though the score is the same. In a similar way, romantic love is played out slightly differently in different cultures. In the West it is marked by special features not found elsewhere. These special features include the idea that romantic love must take you by surprise, the idea that it should be the basis for a lifelong commitment, and the idea that it is the supreme form of self-fulfilment. So, while romantic love is a universal theme, it is a theme that admits of some minor variations.

Romantic love may not be a culturally specific emotion like 'being a wild pig', but nor is it a basic emotion like fear. The philosopher Paul Griffiths has argued that there are not two kinds of emotion, but three. In addition to basic emotions and culturally specific emotions, he claims that there are 'higher cognitive emotions'. This is fine, so long as we realize that these categories are not black and white. As already noted, the distinction between basic emotions and culturally specific emotions is one of degree rather than of kind. There is a spectrum of innateness, with basic emotions being located at the 'very innate' end, and culturally specific emotions at the 'least innate' end. Adding a third category called 'higher cognitive emotions' is to divide the spectrum up into three sections rather than two. Higher cognitive emotions are less innate than basic emotions, but more innate than culturally specific ones.

As well as differing from basic emotions in their degree of innateness, higher cognitive emotions also differ in a number of other ways. They are not so automatic and fast as basic emotions, and nor are they universally associated with a single facial expression. Love is a case in point. Although love at first sight is possible, it is relatively rare; it seems much more common for love to grow gradually over the space of several days, weeks, or even months. Contrast this with the emotion of fear, which typically overtakes a person in a matter of milliseconds. And, while fear is easily recognizable by its typical facial expression, there is no specific facial expression associated with the emotion of love.

Griffiths proposes that emotions like love should be called 'higher cognitive emotions', because they involve much more cortical processing than basic emotions. While basic emotions are largely processed in sub-cortical structures buried beneath the surface of the brain, emotions like love are more associated with areas of the neocortex. The neocortex is the part of the brain that has expanded most in the past five million years of human evolution, and supports most of our most complex cognitive abilities such as explicit logical analysis. The fact that the higher cognitive emotions are more cortical than the basic emotions means that they are more capable of being influenced by conscious thoughts, and this in turn is probably what allows higher cognitive emotions to be more culturally variable than the basic emotions. However, despite their greater cultural variability, the higher cognitive emotions are still universal. Like basic emotions, but unlike

Higher cognitive emotions

Higher cognitive emotions are universal, like basic emotions, but they exhibit more cultural variation. They also take longer to build up, and longer to die away, than basic emotions. Higher cognitive emotions include the following:

- Love
- Guilt
- Shame
- Embarrassment
- Pride
- Envy
- Jealousy

Some *basic* emotions can also be co-opted for the social functions that typify *higher cognitive* emotions. When someone feels disgusted by the sight of faeces, this is a basic emotion. When you feel disgusted by an immoral act, however, the basic emotional response designed to keep you away from infectious or poisonous things is co-opted for the *social* function of keeping you away from untrustworthy people.

culturally specific emotions, the higher cognitive emotions are part of human nature, shaped by our common evolutionary history.

What other higher cognitive emotions are there, besides love? Possible candidates include guilt, shame, embarrassment, pride, envy, and jealousy (see Box above). Perhaps *amae* is also best classified as a higher cognitive emotion. This list suggests a further property of higher cognitive emotions: all these emotions are fundamentally *social* in a way that basic emotions are not. You can be afraid of, or disgusted by, inanimate objects and non-human animals, but love and guilt require other people for their existence. You might feel guilty about hurting an animal, and some people claim to be in love with their pets, but it seems unlikely that guilt and love evolved for such purposes. The higher cognitive emotions seem to have been designed by natural selection precisely to help our ancestors cope with an increasingly complex social environment. As we will see in the next chapter, these emotions may be the cement that binds human society together.

Why Spock could never have evolved

If you ever watched *Star Trek*, you'll remember Spock, the pointy-eared alien. Spock was half human and half Vulcan—a species of alien that, by some quirk of fate, happened to look remarkably human in all respects other than those tell-tale ears.

The visual similarity, however, concealed a deeper difference. Behind the human-like face lay an alien brain, far superior to ours. In particular, the Vulcan race had no emotions. At some point in their past, the Vulcans had dispensed with these primitive vestiges of their animal origins, and, no longer encumbered by passion, they had attained a superhuman degree of rationality.

In supposing that a creature devoid of emotions would be more intelligent than we are, the creators of *Star Trek* were perpetuating an ancient theme of Western culture. Ever since Plato, many Western thinkers have tended to view emotions as obstacles to intelligent

5 Leonard Nimoy as Mr Spock in *Star Trek II. The Wrath of Khan*, 1982.

action, or, at best, as harmless luxuries. I call this the negative view of emotion.

The opposite idea—the positive view of emotion—is the view that emotions are vital for intelligent action. According to the positive view of emotion, a creature like Spock, who lacked emotion, would actually be *less* intelligent than we are, not more. Until recently, this idea has not been popular among philosophers and psychologists, but considerations drawn from evolutionary theory and neuroscience now seem to add support to the positive view.

It is easy to find examples to support the negative view of emotion. We are all familiar with cases in which an excess of emotion prevents people from acting intelligently. A man who is insulted by a gang of hooligans would be safer if he ignored the insult and walked away, but his pride may lead him to answer back and thus become the victim of a violent assault. A woman who is criticized by her boss may become upset and walk out of her job, when the most intelligent response may be to ·bite her lip and modify her behaviour. And so on.

It would be stupid to deny that emotions can lead people to do things that they later regret. The positive view of emotions does not hold that emotions are *always* useful. Rather, it maintains (*contra* the negative view of emotion) that the best recipe for success is a mixture of

6 The negative view of emotion.

reason and emotion, not reason alone. Someone who lacked emotions altogether, like Spock, would be better off than us in some circumstances, but worse off in others. Overall, however, the benefits of having emotions far outweigh the drawbacks.

If the advantages of having emotions *never* outweighed the disadvantages, emotional creatures would never have evolved in the first place. Emotions are complex traits, and such traits rarely evolve unless they convey some advantage. So the fact that we have emotions now means that, at some point in our evolutionary history at least, they must have helped our ancestors to survive and procreate. The question is—how?

The value of basic emotions

It is easy to see how some of the basic emotions such as fear and anger helped our ancestors to survive. The capacity for fear is very useful in a world where hungry predators lurk in every shadow. It allows animals to react very swiftly to any possible sign of danger, pumping their bodies full of hormones that facilitate a fast escape and flooding their minds with one thought: flee! (See Box below.) Anger is similar, except that it prepares the organism for a fight rather than for flight.

Surprise and disgust are also fairly easy to decipher. The emotion of surprise helps animals to respond to novel stimuli. When something unexpected comes along, the surprise reaction stops us in our tracks and forces us to pay attention to it. Our eyebrows arch, allowing the eyes to widen and take in as much of the new scene as possible. The body readies itself for a possible change in direction. Likewise, the capacity for disgust is helpful in a world where rotting food and

The two routes to fear

The American neuroscientist Joseph LeDoux has found that fear is controlled by two separate pathways in the brain. The first of these corresponds to the basic emotion. It is very quick, but often makes mistakes. The second is slower, but more accurate. Ideally, the two pathways work together to get us the best of both worlds. The first pathway makes us respond quickly to signs of potential danger, but can often be set off by false alarms. Meanwhile, the second pathway considers the situation more carefully, and if it concludes that the danger is not real, it cuts off the fear response initiated by the first pathway. In phobias, the second pathway ceases to function properly, so that we continue to react fearfully to harmless stimuli.

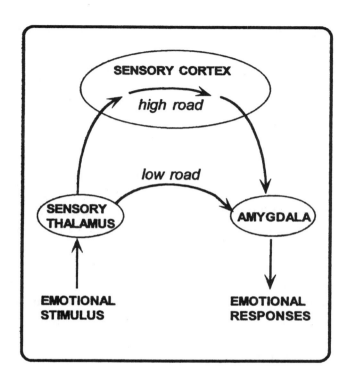

7 The two neural pathways of fear (from *The Emotional Brain*, by Joseph LeDoux).

faeces are homes to colonies of infectious bacteria. By causing animals to steer clear of such objects, disgust helps them to avoid being poisoned or infected.

The evolutionary rationale for the other two basic emotions—joy and distress—is more complex. They almost certainly evolved to act as motivators leading us to pursue or avoid certain courses of action. Joy is produced by actions and events that, in the stone age, would have helped us to pass on our genes. The reason why having sex, meeting old friends, and receiving gifts make us joyful is that all these things were conducive to the reproductive success of our ancestors. Conversely, the reason why the death of a friend or the loss of an important possession are so distressing is that these things were bad for the reproductive success of our ancestors. This does not mean that our ancestors made the connection in their minds between these emotions and genetic success. Natural selection did not design our minds to think directly about how best to pass on our genes. Instead, it gave us the capacity to feel joy, and then made the experience of joy contingent on doing the things that help our genes to get into the next generation.

If joy and distress really evolved to function as motivators, like the proverbial carrot and stick, they must work by anticipation. Without an ability to predict whether a particular course of action will lead us to feel joyful or distressed, these emotions could not provide us with a motive for or against taking that course of action. There would be no point in feeling joyful or distressed if we could not use the anticipation of such feelings to help us decide what to do. This means that we must first experience such feelings willy-nilly in order to learn what things make us joyful or distressed. Only afterwards can we use the memory of such feelings to run our lives. Hence the importance of childhood, the trial period when we discover our personal likes and dislikes.

Fortunately, we do not have to rely entirely on our own experience. Although preferences differ from person to person, the fundamental causes of joy and distress are common to us all, so we can learn from other people's experiences. The same applies to other basic emotions such as fear and disgust. Children who see that their parents are afraid of bathing in a particular river can infer that the river is dangerous without having to test it out for themselves. Likewise, children who see that their parents react with disgust to a particular kind of food can save themselves the trouble of tasting something horrible. In a social species like *Homo sapiens*, then, emotions are doubly useful. On the one hand, the internal feelings and the bodily changes of emotion cause the organism to pursue or avoid particular courses of action. On the other hand, the external expressions of emotion provide information to others, allowing them to learn from our experiences.

The same phenomenon occurs in other social species, including many primates. In one experiment, rhesus macaques reared in a laboratory were unafraid of snakes when they were first exposed to them. However, after watching a film of another monkey reacting to a snake with fear, they too began to show the fear response to snakes. There are limits, however, to this kind of learning from experience. When shown films of other monkeys being frightened by a flower or a rabbit, the laboratory-reared macaques did not develop fears of such harmless things. Emotional learning is a combination of environmental inputs, and an innate disposition to learn some things rather than others.

Not all emotional expressions are designed to allow other animals to learn vicariously. Some emotional expressions are not honest signals of the underlying emotion, but acts of deception. When a cat is frightened, for example, its fur stands on end. The function of this expression is not to let other animals know that the cat is frightened, however. On the contrary, there are some other animals—predators—that the cat would prefer *not* to know it was frightened, since

8 When a cat is frightened, its fur stands on end, which makes it look bigger to potential attackers.

that might encourage them to attack. The purpose of the hair standing on end is to make the cat seem bigger than it really is, and hence to deter predators or other cats from attacking.

When considering the evolution of the emotions, then, we must take into consideration all the elements of each emotional response. It is not enough to focus on the internal feelings; we must also consider the facial expressions and other signals. Darwin was the first to emphasize the importance of these signals, and his book *The Expression of the Emotions in Man and Animals* (1872), examines the continuity of many of them over long stretches of evolutionary time. Darwin was interested in these expressions, because he thought they were good evidence that humans had descended from other animals. He argued, for example, that the way our hair stands on end when we are scared is a leftover from a time when our ancestors were completely covered in fur. Our ancestors would puff up their fur when scared for the same reasons that cats still do today. Now, of course, a few hairs standing up on our heads are unlikely to make us look much bigger, so the reaction has become much less pronounced, but it is still there nonetheless, a legacy of our prehuman ancestors.

The evolutionary causes of emotional expressions such as hair standing on its end in fear, or baring one's teeth in anger, are easy to divine. Other emotional expressions, however, are extremely mysterious. Tears are one such expression. The question of why we cry when distressed has baffled evolutionists. Emotional tears are uniquely human. Most mammals have tear glands, but these exist purely to protect the eye against injury. No other species cries when it is distressed—not even our closest relative, the chimpanzee.

Darwin denied that tears shed in distress served any useful function. The tear glands, he argued, evolved as a means of protecting the eyes in infancy, when prolonged screaming might otherwise cause optical damage. Tears shed by adults in distress, thought Darwin, were merely an incidental result of pressure exerted on the tear glands by screwing up the eyes, just as contraction of the same muscles can lead to tears when you laugh or sneeze.

More recently, this view has been challenged by researchers who have proposed a variety of functions for emotional tears. After finding that tears shed in distress have a different biochemical composition from other kinds of tears, William Frey has suggested that such tears remove stress hormones from the body. This, he claims, is the reason why people usually feel better after having had a good cry. A more common view is that tears provide an honest signal of distress. For signals to be honest, they must be hard to fake, and it does indeed seem very difficult to cry on purpose; it takes a lot of practice before actors can do it convincingly. According to this view, the reason we usually feel better after crying has nothing to do with getting rid of excess hormones; it is simply because crying usually prompts other people to offer us their support. For this to be a plausible evolutionary explanation, of course, crying must have evolved after the emotion of sympathy, or co-evolved in tandem with it. One problem with this theory, however, is that it does not explain why crying *on your own* can sometimes make you feel better.

As humans are the only animals that cry when distressed, this particular emotional expression must have evolved relatively recently, some time after the human lineage diverged from the chimpanzee lineage. Most other emotional expressions are much older. The tendency for our hair to stand on end when we are afraid probably originated over fifty million years ago, when the common ancestor of mammals prowled the earth. The emotion of fear itself is even older than this·particular physiological expression. In fact, fear is probably one of the first emotions ever to have evolved. It is likely to have been present in the first vertebrates, which appeared some 500 million years ago or more. All animals descended from these early vertebrates—

amphibians, reptiles, birds, and mammals—have inherited the capacity for fear. Humans are far from unique in this respect.

Other basic emotions such as joy and distress may have come later, but they are still very old, and thus shared by many animals other than humans. Who can doubt that a cat curled up by a warm fire is feeling its own kind of joy when it purrs so loudly? Evidence for the capacity of non-human animals to feel distress is perhaps harder to come by, but it is difficult to resist the impression that elephants, at least, feel this emotion. Mother elephants are often reluctant to abandon the corpses of their children when they have been slain by hunters, despite the danger this puts them in, and they often return to the proverbial elephants' graveyard.

Before you accuse me of sentimentality, consider the evidence from neuroanatomy. When you compare the brains of widely differing animals, the similarities are striking. In all vertebrates, for example, the brain is divided into three distinct parts known as the hind-brain, midbrain, and forebrain, and within each of these divisions one can find the same basic structures and pathways. This shows that brain evolution is a very conservative process, in which many systems undergo remarkably little modification even though the rest of the body might change dramatically. This is especially true of the neural systems that mediate basic emotions such as fear and anger. The neuroscientist Joseph LeDoux has shown that the same neural mechanisms mediate the fear response in all sorts of animals, from pigeons and rats to cats and humans. The idea that other animals experience similar emotions to us is not anthropomorphism: it is based on sound scientific evidence.

In all mammals, including ourselves, basic emotions such as fear and anger are mediated by a set of neural structures known as the limbic system. These include the hippocampus, the cingulate gyrus, the anterior thalamus, and the amygdala (see Fig. 9). All these structures are tucked away in the centre of the brain, underneath the outer layer of neural tissue known as the neocortex. The neocortex is, as the name suggests, much more recent in evolutionary terms. While there is a kind of neocortex in the brains of fish, amphibians, birds, and reptiles, in mammals it is very much larger and completely envelops the limbic structures. The much larger neocortex is, indeed, the main difference between the brains of mammals and those of other vertebrates. According to the neuroscientist Paul MacLean, the evolution of the mammalian brain consisted mainly in the expansion of the neocortex, while the older limbic structures were much less modified,

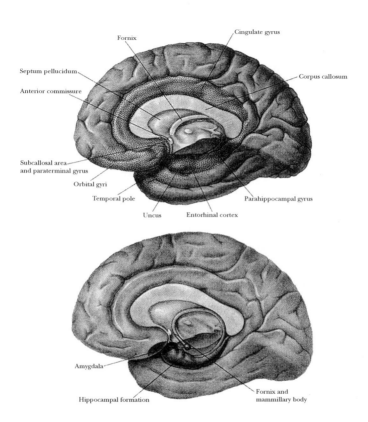

9 The human brain, with some of the limbic structures highlighted.

though of course the latter did not remain *exactly* the same. In making these cross-species comparisons, everything is a question of degree; my limbic structures are different from those of a tortoise (I hope), but my cortex differs much more from the tortoise cortex.

If basic emotions like fear are mediated exclusively by the limbic system, the higher cognitive emotions such as love and guilt seem to involve much more cortical processing. This would suggest that they evolved much later than basic emotions, some time after the point when the neocortex began to expand with the emergence of the higher mammals. In other words, higher cognitive emotions could be no more than sixty million years old, which is very young compared to the 500 or so million years for which the vertebrate brain—and the basic emotions—have been around. In fact, they may well be much *more* recent than that.

The evolution of guilt, love, and revenge

If the time when higher cognitive emotions such as guilt and love first evolved is still rather unclear, the reason why they evolved is even more obscure. It is easy to see how the capacity for fear or disgust helped our ancestors to survive, but it is much harder to understand what benefits they gained by falling in love, or feeling guilty. Yet a number of intriguing suggestions have been put forward that might explain why these emotions, too, are very useful things to have. These suggestions are still largely speculative, so they should be taken with a pinch of salt, but they do provide some further insights into the possible benefits of having emotions.

Take guilt. On the face of it, it is hard to see why natural selection would have endowed us with this emotion. There are many occasions in life when it is possible to cheat—to take a benefit without paying the corresponding price. If you can be reasonably sure that you can cheat without being detected, the most advantageous thing to do is to cheat. If you have a conscience, however, the thought of the guilt that you would feel afterwards might prevent you from cheating. Thus it seems that an animal with the capacity for guilt would be outcompeted by less scrupulous rivals. The capacity for guilt would be eliminated by natural selection.

This analysis has been challenged by the economist Robert Frank. Frank argues that it is actually advantageous to have the capacity for guilt, because people who are known to have a conscience are more likely to be trusted by others. He tells the following story to illustrate his point. Consider two people, Smith and Jones, who wish to start a restaurant. Smith is a talented cook and Jones is a shrewd manager, so together they can launch a successful joint venture that pays each of them more than they would gain from working alone. Yet each of them knows that the other will have opportunities to cheat without being detected. Smith can take kickbacks from food suppliers, for example, while Jones can fiddle the accounts. If only one of them cheats, he will do very well, while the other does poorly. But if both of them cheat, each will do worse than they would do if both were honest. If Smith and Jones could each make a binding commitment not to cheat, both would profit by doing so. But how can they make such a commitment in a way that is credible? Simply promising not to cheat is not convincing; for unscrupulous people, promises are easy to make and just as easy to break.

Here is where guilt comes in handy. If you feel guilty whenever you cheat, this can lead you to behave honestly even when you know that you could get away with cheating. And, if others know that you are this kind of person, they will seek you out as a partner in joint ventures that require trust. This depends, of course, on there being reliable cues that indicate the presence of guilt. Only if there is some reliable signal that you have a conscience, such as blushing when you feel guilty, will others be able to tell the difference between a trustworthy person and a scoundrel. These signals must be hard to fake, otherwise they would not be reliable. Frank argues that some emotional expressions, such as blushing, have been built into human physiology by natural selection precisely to serve as such reliable signals of trustworthiness.

There are lots of other situations in life when it is vital to be able to make credible promises. Frank refers to all these situations as 'commitment problems', and argues that all the higher cognitive emotions solve different kinds of commitment problem. The capacity for guilt solves those commitment problems in which you have to make a credible promise not to cheat. Likewise, argues Frank, romantic love solves another kind of commitment problem—that in which you have to make a credible promise to remain faithful to one other person. Jack and Jill may consider each other suitable mates, but they will be reluctant to commit themselves to each other unless each is sure that the other will not walk out as soon as someone more attractive comes along. The realization that the other person is in love can provide this assurance. If Jack commits himself to Jill because of an emotion he did not 'decide' to have (and so cannot decide *not* to have), an emotion that is reliably indicated by such physiological signals as tachy-cardia and insomnia, then Jill will be more likely to believe he will stay with her than if he had chosen her after coolly weighing up her good and bad points. 'People who are sensible about love are incapable of it,' wrote Douglas Yates.

Another commitment problem involves making credible threats of retaliation. Suppose you are the smallest child in the class, and the class bully threatens to steal your packed lunch. You might threaten to retaliate by punching the bully on the nose, but, if the bully knows you are a rational person, he will not take your threat very seriously. After all, punching the bully on the nose will probably lead to a fight that you would almost certainly lose, and you would then be even worse off, having lost your lunch *and* gained a black eye or two. If, however, you have a reputation for vengeance, then your problem is solved. The impulse to seek revenge will cause you to retaliate after insults, regardless of the consequences, so the bully will think twice about stealing your sandwiches. Once again, emotions seem to exhibit a kind of 'global rationality' that saves pure reason from itself.

According to Frank, then, higher cognitive emotions such as guilt, love, and the impulse to seek revenge all perform very useful functions. They all help us to solve commitment problems that we would be incapable of solving by reason alone. However, these emotions are not without their disadvantages. They may help us to make credible promises and threats, but what if someone calls our bluff? If, despite my racing pulse and reddening face, my declarations of love fall on deaf ears, I will be condemned to several weeks, months, or perhaps even years of useless suffering. Unrequited love is surely one of nature's cruellest punishments. Likewise, if the school bully goes ahead and steals my sandwiches despite being aware of my taste for vengeance, my retaliation will lead me to be even worse off than before, losing my sandwiches *and* acquiring a rather nasty bruise.

It would be nice, of course, if we could obtain the benefits of these emotions without incurring the dangers that ensue when someone calls our bluff. It would be great, for example, if we could make sincere declarations of love that suddenly vanished when our advances were spurned. Or if we could make credible threats of retaliation that melted into timidity whenever someone decided to take us at our word. But to behave in this way would undermine the credibility of any promises and threats we might make in the future. To make a credible threat, you must show that you are somehow *forced* to carry it out. It seems that the higher cognitive emotions cannot avoid being double-edged swords.

Promises and threats are credible only if there is

some evidence that you will carry them out even if it costs you to do so. You must show that you are 'handcuffed' in some way to the execution of the threat or promise. Let us call this the 'handcuff principle'. For these emotions to work, they must have a kind of inevitability built into them, such that, when someone calls your bluff, you cannot avoid carrying out your promise or threat. These emotions handcuff you to a particular course of action that you would rather not carry out. Furthermore, this handcuff must be clearly visible to others. There is no point in having such a mechanism if others cannot see it. In the case of guilt, the handcuff is visibly indicated by physiological cues such as blushing. Most of the time, one hopes, the visibility of the handcuff deters people from calling your bluff. The school bully sees that you are prey to bouts of righteous anger, and leaves your sandwiches alone. But, occasionally, the deterrent fails. The bully steals your sandwiches anyway, leaving you with no choice but to take revenge. The desire for revenge then kicks in, impelling you to punch the bully on the nose. The voice of reason, calling for caution, is swamped by the tide of passion.

When both parties in a dispute are each handcuffed in the same way, another danger arises. In such situations, it needs only one party to call the other's bluff to set off a potentially never-ending cycle of tit for tat.

Steven Pinker tells a parable that illustrates this danger. By a fortuitous coincidence, it involves some *real* handcuffs:

> Protesters attempt to block the construction of a nuclear power plant by lying down on the railroad tracks leading to the site. The engineer, being reasonable, has no choice but to stop the train. The railroad company counters by telling the engineer to set the throttle so that the train moves very slowly and then to jump out of the train and walk beside it. The protesters must scramble. Next time the protesters handcuff themselves to the tracks; the engineer does not dare leave the train. But the protesters must be certain the engineer sees them in enough time to stop. The company assigns the next train to a near-sighted engineer.

It is probably this unfortunate logic that lies behind the eternal vendettas between Mafia families in Italy and North America, and motivates the sectarian killings in Northern Ireland and the Middle East. Wherever the force of law is weak, self-perpetuating cycles of attack and revenge are common. They persist even though they are clearly not in the interest of either party, simply because the impulse to seek revenge is etched deep into our biology. The sad fact is that there is a good evolutionary reason for this feature of human nature. Without a taste for revenge, we would be easy to exploit.

During the course of human evolution, the advantages of this emotion have clearly outweighed the costs.

Are Emotions still useful today?

What about now, though? Emotions such as the taste for revenge may have been useful to our hunter-gatherer ancestors, whose vendettas were conducted with sticks and stones and probably led to far fewer fatalities, but they are surely counterproductive in a world in which guns are freely available. Perhaps all emotions are like this. Perhaps the Vulcan race really *is* ahead of us in the evolutionary game. Spock and his fellow Vulcans may have done well to leave their emotions behind when their world became high tech.

This seems to have been Darwin's view, whose book on *The Expression of the Emotions* gives the impression that emotional expressions, while useful in the past, are no longer of any value. In arguing, for example, that the tendency for humans to bare their teeth in anger was a leftover from a primitive agonistic display practised by our pre-human ancestors, Darwin seems to imply that emotional expressions, and by extension the feelings that underlie them, are rather like the appendix—a vestigial organ, derived from an earlier phase of our evolutionary history, which is no longer of any use. Darwin's account thus seems to reinforce the negative view of emotion.

It is true that we live in a world that is very different, in many ways, from the world in which our ancestors lived. We no longer face the constant threat of being eaten by predators, for example, and the chance of being assaulted by other humans is surely much reduced. If the emotion of fear evolved to help us avoid these dangers, then it might seem that we would be better off without it today. Certainly, an excessive capacity for fear leads to all sorts of problems that many people would dearly love to be free of, such as phobias and panic attacks. One does not hear of many people who suffer from the opposite problem—that of having too *little* fear. The reason for this apparent imbalance, however, may well be that those with no capacity for fear wind up in the morgue long before they are aware they have a problem. Fear does not merely protect us against predators. It also deters us from a whole host of reckless behaviours, many of which are potentially fatal. Fear will stop you from crossing a busy road without looking, or from dancing on the edge of a cliff. A life without fear might be less painful, but it would also be a lot shorter.

Anger, too, would seem to be rather useless today.

Unlike our pre-human ancestors, most of us do not regularly engage in physical violence, so what is the benefit of conserving an emotional capacity whose function is to help us fight? One answer is that fighting need not be a physical affair. Our disputes are carried on by other means today, but they still require grit and determination, and anger provides just such internal motivation. People who never get angry never get ahead. Moreover, we should not exaggerate the degree to which the need for physical violence has disappeared from our world. There are still many times, even in the affluent and law-abiding cultures of the developed world, when resorting to physical violence is the only way to defend oneself. The film *Demolition Man* is set in the future, at a time when the human capacity for anger has completely atrophied. When a vicious criminal appears on the scene, resuscitated from the state of suspended animation to which he was condemned in the twentieth century, nobody is able to deal with him. The criminal is caught only following the revival of another twentieth-century human, a policeman who, like the criminal, still possesses the capacity for anger.

It is much easier to see that too much anger causes problems too. Road rage is an obvious example. In some Western countries in recent years there has been a growing number of such incidents. Worn down by the stress of driving on increasingly crowded roads, some drivers reach a point where the smallest annoyance causes them to snap. Sometimes a frustrated driver simply sounds his horn, or swears at the person who has annoyed him. At other times, however, he may jump out of his car and drag the other driver from his seat into the road, where he vents his frustration by punching and kicking him. Anger is useful in the right amount, but when it is excessive it can lead to serious problems.

The same point probably applies to all the other emotions too. The optimal state of an emotion involves having just the right amount of it, neither too little nor too much. Even sexual jealousy probably has an optimal midpoint between extreme possessiveness and extreme permissiveness (see Box below). Aristotle based his whole ethical system around this simple idea. The virtues, he claimed, were all midpoints between the extremes of having too little or too much of a particular emotion. Courage was the midpoint between the extremes of having too much or too little fear. The virtue of amiability lay halfway between the extremes of cantankerousness and obsequiousness. And so on.

Aristotle's concept of the golden mean is remarkably similar to what psychologists now refer to as 'emotional intelligence'. Emotional intelligence involves striking a balance between emotion and reason in which neither

Jealousy: good or bad?

Like other higher cognitive emotions, jealousy evolved to help our ancestors survive and reproduce in complex social groups. By prompting them to keep a watchful eye over their mates, jealousy helped our ancestors to make sure that their sexual partners were not defaulting on the cooperative venture of having and raising children. As with other emotions, however, too much can be a bad thing. Too much jealousy can lead people to be violent and coercive, which can drive the partner away or even result in his or her death. Stalkers are usually jilted lovers whose jealousy leads them to pursue their former partners with inappropriate and frightening zeal. Such examples of jealousy gone wrong can easily tempt us into thinking that all jealousy is bad. This is to throw the baby out with the bath water. Too much jealousy is a bad thing, but so is too little. How many people would feel their partner truly loved them if they never showed any signs of jealousy at all?

is completely in control. Emotionally intelligent people know when it is right to control their emotions and when it is right to be controlled by them. Emotional intelligence also involves the ability to read other people's emotions correctly. Guessing other people's

10 A woman looks on with jealousy while a man flirts with some-one else.

emotional state is easy when they are in fits of tears, but the signs are not always so obvious. We often try to mask our emotions, making it harder for others to guess what we are feeling, though we rarely succeed in controlling all the involuntary twitches that betray our inner thoughts. The capacity to gauge someone's mood from such subtle signs is a much rarer talent, though it can be improved with practice.

Evidence is now mounting that the ability to recognize facial expressions of emotion is subserved by specialized neural circuitry. These circuits comprise key limbic structures such as the amygdala. When these structures are damaged, the circuit is broken and the ability to discriminate between different facial expressions of emotion is diminished. Bilateral damage to the amygdala, for example, reduces people's ability to detect negative emotions such as fear and anger. It seems that evolution did not just shape our capacity to feel and express emotions, but also gave us special-purpose mechanisms for emotional recognition.

The usefulness of such machinery should be clear by now. Without the ability to divine the emotions felt by others, we would lose many opportunities to learn from their experience, with the result that we would have to learn everything the hard way—on our own. We would also find it much harder to know whom to trust.

Involuntary emotional signals provide some of the most reliable information about people's characters. In one experiment, strangers were paired at random and given thirty minutes to interact. Then they were asked to make a simple decision, in private, about whether or not they would cooperate with the other person, or cheat. They were also asked to guess what the other person would do. Success rates were remarkably high. The subjects of these experiments all had normal brains; those whose ability to detect emotional cues has been diminished by brain-damage do much worse in similar experimental conditions.

It should be clear by now that a creature totally devoid of any emotional capacity would not survive for very long. Lacking fear, the creature might sit around and ponder whether or not the approaching lion really represented a threat or not. Without anger, it would be picked on mercilessly. Lack of disgust would allow it to consume faeces and rotting food. And without the capacity for joy and distress, it might never bother doing anything at all—not a good recipe for survival. *Star Trek* notwithstanding, the Vulcan race could never have evolved.

Moral sentiments

Even if the Vulcans somehow *did* manage to evolve, they probably would not be very nice. Emotions seem to underlie much, if not all, of our moral behaviour. Without them, we would not be capable of virtue. A long line of thinkers, from Aristotle to Adam Smith, have emphasized the fundamental role of emotion in guiding moral behaviour. I have already mentioned Aristotle's concept of virtue as a midpoint between emotional extremes. Adam Smith also linked emotions to morality, though in a rather different way. He thought that some emotions were designed specifically for the purpose of helping us to behave morally, a view that now seems to be supported by evolutionary theory. Smith referred to these emotions as 'the moral sentiments'.

Other thinkers have taken a very different view of the relationship between emotion and morality. Hobbes thought that our natural emotional inclinations would almost always make us tend towards selfish behaviour, and that the only way for us to behave in a moral fashion was to transcend our animal instincts and act in accordance with the law. A similar view was proposed by Kant. Kant did not deny that emotions could sometimes lead us to do the right thing, but he argued that such emotionally inspired actions were not truly virtuous. If a man obeyed the moral law out of fear, for example, this would not be a case of moral behaviour for Kant. The only way of behaving morally, according to Kant's view, was to obey the moral law completely unemotionally, purely for the sake of obeying the law. This is a bloodless view of morality fit only for Vulcans.

Unfortunately, however, Kant's Vulcan morality has had a great deal of influence on Western thought. On the one hand, it has encouraged a negative view of emotion, so that it is now common to think that acts lose their moral worth when they are inspired by emotion. A classic example of this perverse reasoning was provided by a Conservative politician a few years ago in England. In an attempt to discredit the policies of the Opposition, which aimed at redistributing wealth more equitably among all layers of society, he accused his opponents of preaching 'the politics of envy'. The implicit reasoning is clear: envy is an emotion, and not a very nice one at that, so any policy motivated by it must be similarly bad. But envy is not all bad. In fact, it may prove to be crucial for our sense of justice and for motivating us to build a fairer society; 'envy is the basis of democracy,' wrote Bertrand Russell. It may well have evolved precisely for such purposes, as it was crucial to guard against excessive inequality during most of human evolution when our ancestors lived in small bands of hunter-gatherers. Or it may simply have evolved to motivate people to get more for themselves. Either way, envy is part of human nature, and the politicians cannot legislate it out of existence. All we can do is decide how we express it; either through policies of wealth redistribution, or through violence and theft. Did the Conservative politician think the latter was preferable?

On the other hand, the Kantian view of morality has also given rise to a misleading view of how people make moral decisions. According to a view known as moral law theory, whenever we have to decide which course of action is morally superior, we do so by applying a set of general rules to a particular situation, just like the judges working within a Napoleonic legal system. Ideas like this prompted the philosopher Leibniz to dream about creating a machine that would apply the rules for you, thereby automating all moral decisions and finally removing all uncertainty from our moral life. If we wanted to know whether something was right or wrong, all we would need to do would be to consult our moral computer.

The fantasy of the moral programme still underlies a lot of work in the psychology of moral behaviour today. Theories of how the capacity for moral reasoning develops in children are still largely based on the idea that such development consists in acquiring a set of rules. *Star Trek*, once again, provides us with a personification of this idea, though this time the character is from *Star Trek: The Next Generation* rather than from the original series. Commander Data is an android, a robot so human-like that it is hard to tell the difference between him and us. Inside Data's silicon brain is a specialized bit of software concerned exclusively with moral behaviour. In one episode, this 'ethical subroutine' was disabled, and Data suddenly became inconsiderate and then psychopathic.

Psychopaths are indeed curiously amoral, but this is not because they lack an 'ethical subroutine'. The moral capacities that most of us have, and that psychopaths lack, are based not on a set of rules like the instructions in a computer program, but on emotions like sympathy, guilt, and pride. The development of moral capacities in children is, therefore, not likely to be helped by teaching them a set of commandments or precepts, unless their emotional capacities are also well nurtured. Psychopaths are only too good at applying rules. Without moral sentiments to guide your moral reasoning, you would only ever obey the letter of the law rather than the spirit.

Short cuts to happiness

The range of things that can make us joyful or distressed is simply vast. Witnessing a beautiful sunset, making love, eating an ice cream, and listening to Bach's cantatas are four very different kinds of activity, but they are all capable of inducing joy. On the downside, losing your favourite teddy bear, failing an exam, and hearing about the death of a loved one can all provoke distress. Is there any pattern underlying this bewildering diversity?

In an attempt to answer this question, psychologists have compiled a huge database on what makes people happy. Happiness is not the same as joy, but it is closely linked. Joy is a basic emotion, and, like the other basic emotions, a single episode lasts only a few seconds, rarely more than a minute. Happiness is a mood, and moods last much longer—from several minutes to several hours. Moods are background states that raise or lower our susceptibility to emotional stimuli. In a happy mood, for example, we will be more likely to react joyfully to good news, while, in a sad mood, we might not react so intensely. Conversely, someone in a sad mood is more likely to cry at bad news, while a person in a happy mood might laugh it off. In an anxious mood, we are more easily frightened, while an irritable mood makes us more readily angered.

People are more interested in happiness than joy because happiness lasts longer and makes joy more likely. The joy produced by witnessing a beautiful sunset lasts barely longer than the sunset itself, but the experience may put us in a happy mood that stays with us for hours. When psychologists do research on general life satisfaction, they are investigating happiness, not joy. The World Database of Happiness combines the results of hundreds of surveys that have been carried out on life satisfaction.

Combing through this database, the first thing that leaps out is that material wealth is not a good way to become happy. The old cliché about the impossibility of buying contentment seems to be borne out by the scientific research. Of course, a certain amount of money can help to protect you from some of the most common causes of unhappiness, such as starvation and lack of medical care, but there is more to achieving happiness than simply avoiding pain and hunger.

Many people today, however, cling to the illusion that gaining material wealth will be the key to all their problems. Hence the common dream of winning the lottery.

Such dreams might not be so common if people knew about the studies that have been done on people who really have won lots of money. These studies reveal that most people are not made supremely happy by their winnings. When people win a fortune on the lottery, a few find that their life satisfaction increases, but for most winners the euphoria quickly wears off and they feel exactly as they did before the win. Those who were happy beforehand return to their state of normal happiness. Those who were depressed go back to being depressed.

Getting rich quickly rarely leads to long-term bliss in itself. When the initial high has worn off, a sudden windfall may even *decrease* your happiness. This, at least, was what Adam Smith thought (see Box below), although some recent research casts doubt on this idea. Smith argued that *any* bit of sudden good fortune, monetary or otherwise, was likely to backfire. The story of Johnny Ace is a case in point. Johnny Ace was a rock-'n'-roll star who shot to fame when his first single reached number one in 1952. His next three records were all instant hits too. Suddenly, this obscure

11 'It could be you' proclaims this poster advertising the British National Lottery, playing on the illusion that material wealth will bring lifelong happiness.

preacher's son had become a rock star. Then his luck ran out. His fifth single was successful, but not quite as much as the previous ones. His sixth record did not even get into the charts. On Christmas Eve 1954, Johnny put a revolver to his head and blew his brains out. According to one account, he was just clowning about with the gun. It seems more likely, however, that the sudden rise to fame left him ill prepared for the setbacks that most other musicians get used to dealing with early on in their careers.

If material wealth and sudden good fortune do not lead to happiness, what does? According to the happiness database, the things that are most likely to make you happy are the things we have known about all along: good health, good friends, and, above all, good family relationships. Getting on well with parents, children, and partners is the key to a happy life. Falling in love and having a child that you want are the events most likely to bring lasting joy. Once again, the old clichés are remarkably accurate.

If happiness is mainly about getting and keeping good relationships, sadness is linked with failing to achieve good relationships and losing them. Losing a lot of money will make you sad, but losing a loved one will make you even sadder. If sadness is always about loss, the most painful losses involve other people: the

Adam Smith on the perils of
good fortune

'The man who, by some sudden revolution of fortune, is lifted up at once into a condition of life, greatly above what he had formerly lived in, may be assured that the congratulations of his best friends are not all of them perfectly sincere. An upstart, though of the greatest merit, is generally disagreeable, and a sentiment of envy commonly prevents us from heartily sympathising with his joy. If he has any judgement, he is sensible of this, and instead of appearing to be elated with his good fortune, he endeavours, as much as he can, to smother his joy, . . . It is seldom that with all of this he succeeds. We suspect the sincerity of his humility, and he grows weary of this constraint. In a little time, therefore, he generally leaves all of his old friends behind him, some of the meanest among them excepted, who may, per-haps, condescend to become his dependents: nor does he always acquire any new ones; the pride of his new connections is as much affronted by finding him their equal, as that of his old ones had been by his becoming their superior: and it requires the most obstinate and persevering modesty to atone for this mortification to either. He generally grows weary too soon, and is pro-voked, by the sullen and suspicious pride of the one, and by the saucy contempt of the other, to treat the first with neglect, and the second with petulance, till at last he grows habitually insolent, and forfeits the esteem of all. If the chief part of human happiness arises from the consciousness of being beloved, as I believe it does, those sudden changes of fortune seldom contribute much to happiness. He is happiest who advances more gradually to greatness . . . '

Source: Adam Smith,
The Theory of Moral Sentiments (1759)

moment when a child leaves home, the betrayal of a friendship, the death of a partner.

In the previous chapter we saw that the emotions of joy and distress evolved to act as motivators, like an internal carrot and stick. The moods of happiness and sadness may work in a similar way. Natural selection did not design our minds to think directly about how best to pass on our genes. Instead, it gave us the capacity to feel happy, and then it made the experience of happiness contingent on doing the things that help our genes to get into the next generation. The reason that falling in love makes us happy is that those of our ancestors who liked falling in love were more likely to pass on their genes than those who preferred solitude.

This works only if the things that make us happy are also the things that assist genetic replication. For millions of years, this was the case. In the stone age and before, the only way for our ancestors to be happy was by doing the things that helped them to pass on their genes, such as having friends and lovers. In the past few thousand years, however, the development of technology has changed all that. Alone among all animal species, humans have invented artificial means of inducing pleasurable moods. These technologies of mood short-circuit the routes to happiness designed by natural selection. Instead of wasting months or years looking for a romantic partner, we can get an instant high by taking a drug. In order to be happy, we no longer need to do the things that help us pass on our genes. It appears we have outsmarted natural selection.

Talkin' blues

The first technology of mood our ancestors discovered was language. People have used language in various ways to induce happiness artificially, ways that offer no obvious genetic benefits. I will mention three: consoling, entertaining, and 'venting'. The first two methods benefit the hearer; the last is supposed to benefit the speaker.

Our ancestors probably consoled each other with

hugs and caresses long before they learned how to talk, but once language was invented they found a new way of providing consolation by offering words of sympathy and advice. In doing so, they discovered that words can be powerful antidepressants. This practice has been around so long that it is now almost instinctual. Faced with friends who are feeling down, we all naturally find ourselves trying to talk them out of it. We also naturally administer the same linguistic medicine to ourselves, whispering silent words of encouragement to ourselves when we are low. Cognitive therapy, a form of psychotherapy pioneered by Aaron Beck in the 1960s, is based on just this kind of internal monologue. While cognitive therapy may be original in the way it tries to formalize this process, the practice of talking oneself up is probably as old as language itself.

By teaching people to identify their negative thoughts and replace them with more positive ones, cognitive therapists hope to allow people to become the masters of their emotions rather than their slaves. The idea behind this is an old one, going right back to Aristotle, who pointed out that emotions both influence, and are influenced by, the thoughts we have (more on this in the next chapter). By training ourselves to eliminate thoughts that provoke bad moods and to encourage thoughts that foster pleasant emotions, we may be able to gain some measure of control over our emotional state and lift ourselves out of the blues by sheer will power. But this may not always be possible. Sometimes, the intensity of the emotion may not permit alternative thoughts to be entertained, which is why cognitive therapy does not always work. For someone who is slightly blue, it may help to suggest alternative ways of looking at her situation. But for someone in the grip of a severe depression, such suggestions may appear rather glib. Telling a suicidal person to think positively is not a very effective way to cheer him up.

Cognitive therapy does not merely make such glib suggestions, but rather teaches specific techniques for identifying and eliminating negative thoughts. When administered by a trained therapist, it can be as effective in treating depression as certain drugs like Prozac. Despite the claims for the specific techniques of cognitive therapy, however, I wonder whether most of its efficacy is due not to the advice given by the therapist, but to the expression of sympathy.

Another way of using language to cheer someone up is by telling stories and jokes. Stories appeal to our evolved appetite for social information, but manage to satisfy that appetite despite the fact that they are untrue. This is rather odd from an evolutionary point of view. If language evolved, as some people have argued, to enable our ancestors to swap information about other members of the social group, then we should expect the emotional satisfaction that arises from obtaining such information to be contingent on believing it to be true. There are not many evolutionary advantages to be gained from pursuing and taking delight in false information. Yet this is exactly what seems to underlie the universal human love of fiction and drama. The evolutionary benefits of our sense of humour, to which jokes appeal, are even more mysterious. Geoffrey Miller proposes that stories and jokes delight us because they do, in fact, provide useful information—information about the intelligence of the narrator. When someone makes up a story, he is calling attention to his own creativity. When someone tells us a joke, he is displaying his understanding of what makes others laugh. So perhaps telling stories and jokes are not really technologies either, but instincts.

A third linguistic technology of emotion is venting. Venting means talking about unpleasant emotions in order to make them go away. Unlike consolation and entertainment, which may be as old as language itself, venting is a relatively recent invention. People have probably used language to 'get things off their chest' for thousands of years, but venting is more than just unburdening yourself of a troublesome thought. It is the use of language for the explicit purpose of getting rid of unpleasant emotions. The idea of venting was largely pioneered by the Viennese physician Sigmund Freud (1859–1939), who argued that speaking about negative emotions was sometimes the *only* way to be rid of them. To understand how Freud arrived at this view, it is necessary to digress a little and look at the 'hydraulic theory' of emotion on which Freud's arguments seem to rest.

Hydraulics is the science of conveying liquids through pipes and channels, and the hydraulic theory of emotion views feelings as mental fluids that circulate around the mind, much as the blood courses through the veins. Whenever you hear someone telling you not to 'bottle your feelings up', or warning you that you will 'burst under pressure', they are implicitly endorsing this view. As some liquids can easily be converted into vapours, gaseous metaphors such as 'letting off steam' can also be pressed into the service of the hydraulic theory.

The hydraulic theory of emotion goes back at least as far as the French philosopher and scientist René Descartes (1596–1650). Descartes envisaged the nerves as pneumatic pipes, transmitting the pressure of 'animal spirits' from nerve endings to the brain, and thence to the muscles. This was very much in line with humoral theory, which dominated medical thinking in the West from the time of the Greeks until the eighteenth century. According to this theory, the most important determinants of health were the four 'humours' found in the body: blood, phlegm, black bile, and yellow bile. Most illnesses were thought to result from imbalances or blockages in these liquids, which is why bloodletting was such a popular treatment for many disorders during the past two millennia.

Once Descartes had proposed that the mind also functioned by means of hydraulic principles, it was perhaps inevitable that the humoral theory of medicine would be extended from bodily disease to mental disorder. This, in essence, was what Freud did when he invented psychoanalysis. Freud argued explicitly that, since the mind was constantly being replenished with its mental fluid, the libido, it would have to be 'bled' in much the same way as doctors bled the diseased body. Emotional expression was the normal means by which the mental fluid was discharged, but, if emotional expression was inhibited, the fluid would seek discharge via another outlet, which might be dangerous.

The moral that Freud drew from this reasoning was that the inhibition of natural emotional expressions could lead to dangerous consequences. If you are angry, and you do not vent the anger directly, it will not just go away. If the anger is not discharged via its natural outlet, such as shouting at the person who annoyed you, it will well up inside you like some noxious fluid, until eventually you blow your top at someone who really does not deserve it. If all such expression were inhibited, Freud thought that the emotion would then seek discharge through other, even less palatable, outlets, such as symptoms of a psychosomatic nature. Luckily, argued Freud, there were other ways to 'get it out of your system', such as talking to a psychotherapist, that would allow a dangerous build-up of emotion to be vented without transgressing social norms or making yourself ill.

The idea that talking about your feelings functions as a kind of safety valve, allowing psychic pressure to be vented just as excess steam is allowed to escape from a blocked pipe, is sometimes referred to as the 'cathartic theory' of emotion. Anything that allows you to 'get it out of your system' is called a 'cathartic' experience. Catharsis is a Greek term, and plays a central role in Aristotle's *Poetics*, but the word had a very different meaning then. It certainly had nothing to do with the hydraulic theory of emotion. The current usage of the term goes back to Freud, who used it to describe the discharge of his hypothetical 'mental fluid'. In so doing, Freud unwittingly fostered the mistaken belief that the hydraulic theory of emotion goes back to Ancient Greece. Nothing could be further from the truth. There is still some dispute about what exactly Aristotle meant by catharsis, but we know that it was not about 'letting off steam'. The philosopher Martha Nussbaum has argued that it was a fairly intellectual activity, in which the relation of emotions to human action was clarified by a process of experience and reflection. According to Aristotle, the theatre was the perfect place to practise catharsis, perhaps because it allows us to experience emotions at what Thomas Scheff has called 'a best aesthetic distance'. If we are caught up directly in a powerful emotion, it may be too overwhelming for us to learn from the experience. Conversely, if we are too distant from an emotional event, it will not touch us at all. The function of drama may be to provide us with a context in which emotions may be experienced at a safe distance so that we may learn how to deal with them better in the future.

So, if the hydraulic theory of emotion is not an Ancient Greek idea, and has little to do with Aristotle's idea of catharsis, where does it come from? As already noted, it has elements that can be traced back to the humoral theory of disease and Descartes's view of nerves as pneumatic pumps. However, the idea that the *verbal* expression of emotion functions like a safety valve is much more recent. Since Freud popularized the idea at the beginning of the twentieth century, it has grown in popularity until it is now common currency in many Western countries. We look back at the stiff-necked Victorians with a smug sense of superiority. 'Emotional literacy' is held in high esteem. People who cannot talk openly about their feelings are regarded as psychologically immature, relics of a bygone age when repression reigned supreme. However, psychologists are increasingly realizing that the hydraulic theory of emotion is too simplistic. It may well be very good on some occasions to indulge in the spontaneous expression of emotion. On other occasions, however, it can be positively harmful.

Recent evidence has pointed to the possible dangers of talking about one's emotions at the wrong time. The evidence concerns a kind of psychological therapy known as 'debriefing'. Debriefing is given to victims of traumatic events in many Western countries. As soon as there is a major disaster, such as a rail crash or a hijacking, counsellors are flown out to the scene along with the emergency services. After being treated by doctors for physical injury, the victims are treated by the counsellors for 'psychological injury'. The treatment involves going over the memories of the traumatic event and talking through all the feelings they inspire.

Debriefing is quite different in many ways from classical Freudian psychoanalysis, but it is based on the same underlying idea. Like psychoanalysis, debriefing takes a hydraulic view of emotion in assuming that talking about the negative emotions generated by the trauma should allow them to dissipate harmlessly, rather than being bottled up for the future. If the hydraulic view of emotion were correct, we should expect to find that those who undergo debriefing immediately after a traumatic event would suffer fewer long-term symptoms than those who receive no counselling. According to psychologist Jo Rick, however, things are the other way round: debriefing actually makes things worse. In one study of road-accident victims, she found that those who had undergone debriefing had more flashbacks and more fear a year after the accident than those who had not.

In the light of the past few decades of brain research, it is now easy to see why talking about traumatic memories is likely to make things worse rather than better. When left unexamined, bad memories do not fester like some untreated wound, as Freud thought. Rather, they tend to fade away, a process known as 'extinction'. By contrast, if the neural circuits encoding memories are continually reactivated by recounting the original experiences, extinction is prevented. Talking about old memories does not help them to go away. On the contrary, it keeps them alive, as Adam Smith recognized long before neuroscience discovered the process of extinction. In *The Theory of Moral Sentiments*, he noted that, 'by relating their misfortunes', those who seek sympathy 'awaken in their memory the remembrance of those circumstances that occasioned their affliction. Their tears accordingly flow faster than before, and they are apt to abandon themselves to all the weakness of sorrow.'

Evolutionary theory also raises serious questions about the plausibility of the hydraulic model of emotion. The hydraulic model envisions emotions as forces that seek discharge by any means necessary. Just as it does not really matter to the river whether it flows out to the sea by its normal route, or whether it is diverted into another channel, so emotional pressure can be 'released' equally well by a whole variety of different actions ranging from talking and writing to neurotic symptoms and artistic creativity. When you think about it from an evolutionary point of view, this seems an extremely unlikely mental design. Why would natural selection produce such an indeterminate kind of psychic energy? Our minds evolved to solve lots of particular problems, all of which were crucial for survival or reproduction. Any specific action pattern, such as running away, will be good for dealing with some situations, such as encountering an approaching predator, and positively ruinous when dealing with others, such as encountering a potential mate. If different emotions evolved to motivate different kinds of action, it is hard to see why they should 'build up' like some waste product when not 'discharged', let alone why they should be capable of being 'released' by completely unrelated actions.

Language, it seems, is not the most effective short cut to happiness. While a few well-chosen words may at times bring solace, and a good joke may bring on fits of laughter, such things are rarely enough to cure a severe depression. Nor, as we have just seen, is talking about your own bad feelings always the best way to make yourself feel better. For these reasons, humans have constantly sought to discover other technologies of mood that might provide a faster and more secure short cut to happiness than words alone.

The pleasures of the senses

The use of colour is one such technology. For thousands of years, humans have decorated their own bodies and their surroundings with unusually bright colours that stimulate our visual systems much as chocolate stimulates our taste buds. Ever since the discovery of the first artificial dyes, such as the red ochre with which our ancestors painted their bodies around a hundred thousand years ago, we have used bright colours for their emotional effects.

Colour rarely affects our emotions directly. In some mental disorders such as autism the sight of a patch of colour may be enough to trigger a wave of panic, but in most normal people colour influences emotion indirectly via its influence on mood. Being in a red room may not itself make us angry, but it may put us into an irritable mood, with the result that it takes less to make us lose our temper. The Italian film director Michelangelo Antonioni once painted the canteen red to put his actors in the right mood for some tense scenes, but after a few weeks he noticed that other workers using the canteen had become more aggressive and had even come to blows on a few occasions.

Some of the most convincing scientific evidence about the effects of colour on mood comes from some experiments conducted by the psychologist Nicholas Humphrey. Humphrey put monkeys into specially designed cages each consisting of two chambers connected by a tunnel. When one chamber was lit by a blue light and the other by a red light, the monkeys consistently preferred the blue one. They would venture into the red chamber out of curiosity, and then quickly retreat into the blue chamber, where they would remain. If both chambers were red, the monkeys ran back and forth from one chamber to the other, without settling in either. Red made the monkeys irritable and nervous, while blue put them in a relaxed mood.

Red and blue produce similar emotional effects in humans. When people are exposed to red light, blood pressure rises, breathing speeds up, and the heart beats faster. Blue light has the opposite effects. Subjectively, people feel warmer in red rooms but also more nervous and aggressive. These responses are not merely cultural artefacts; two-week-old babies can be soothed more easily in blue than in red light, which suggests that at least part of our emotional response to colour is innate. But why should natural selection have programmed our minds in this way? How could a taste for certain bright colours or an aversion to others possibly have helped our ancestors to survive? Does red owe its warming effect to the fact that the two sources of heat our ancestors had—sunlight and firelight—are both this colour? What about the anxiety-provoking character of red light then? Is this due to the fact that red is also the colour of blood?

Whatever the reason for our innate colour preferences, nature rarely offers us a large expanse of a single colour. A vivid sunset may occasionally paint the whole sky in one consistent shade of pink or purple, but nature's beauties are more usually mosaics of many different colours. A peacock's tail and a beautiful landscape both offer a myriad different shades to the viewer's eye, not a monochromatic expanse like Antonioni's red canteen. By taking a single colour out of its natural setting, and using it to fill the entire visual field, paint and lighting amplify the natural effects of colour. In the technical terms of biology, artificial colours are 'super-stimuli'. They achieve their effects by keying into the same evolved preferences that nature keys into, but they strike the keys much more forcefully. Compared to the neon glow of rococo art, nature is 'too green and badly lit', remarked the painter François Boucher.

A single uniform patch of colour is not always more emotionally powerful than a mosaic, however. What the mosaic loses in simplicity it can gain from careful arrangement. The emotional effects of such arrangements vary much more from person to person than the effects of single colours, so that one painting may produce a profound effect on one person while leaving another person cold. However, there are still some remarkable regularities in our aesthetic preferences. When asked to choose between a selection of abstract paintings, most people prefer the same one. Furthermore, they usually prefer the one painted by a famous artist rather than versions of this that have been modified in random ways by a computer. The original paintings must embody features that the human visual system is programmed to find most appealing. At present, scientists do not know what these features are, but the artists who painted the popular paintings must have had some intuitive appreciation of them. As the landscape painter John Constable remarked, painting is a science of which pictures are but the experiments. Both abstract art and representational art require considerable skill on the part of the artist, even if only in telling the experiments that work from those that do not.

Just as various colours may be arranged to produce a pleasing image, so sounds of varying frequency may be arranged to produce a pleasing melody. Music, like visual art, is a technology designed to tap directly into our perceptual capacities purely for the sake of producing pleasure. In Steven Pinker's words, music is 'auditory cheesecake'; for Shakespeare, music was also the food of love, indicating that music can also induce emotions other than happiness.

Like visual art, music affects our emotions indirectly, by changing our mood. Little scientific research has

12 Music is one of the most powerful technologies of mood we have invented.

been done to find exactly which kinds of music tend to put people in which moods, but most people today know the irritating effects of being exposed to loud, repetitive music from a neighbour's flat or a fellow-passenger's Walkman. Hearing such music does not usually send you into a fit of rage immediately. Rather, it gradually puts you in a bad mood, which then makes you more easily angered. Similarly, supermarkets do not use soft music to make us happy directly; that would rather defeat their objective, since the supermarket bosses do not want you to feel fulfilled by the music itself. Rather, they hope that the music will put you in a relaxed mood, which will in turn make you more sensitive to happiness-inducing thoughts, such as the anticipated pleasure of consuming an expensive chocolate cake.

Among the little scientific research that has been done in this area, one intriguing finding is that many compositions by Mozart, such as *Eine kleine Nachtmusik*, reliably produce good moods in those who hear them. This happens even if the listener is not particularly keen on classical music, which suggests that good composers tap into universal musical preferences in the way that good artists tap into universal visual preferences. Some support for this view can be found in recent neuroscientific research, which has found that, when a person listens to a classical melody, the neurons in different brain regions fire more synchronously than when the person listens to a random sequence of the same notes. The reason for this sense of melody, however, is still a mystery.

In humans, as in other primates, the visual system is highly developed, followed closely by the auditory system. The other sensory modalities are much less complex, or at least we are much less aware of their complexity. So it is not surprising that the sensory technologies of mood we esteem the most—art and music—are those that gratify our eyes and ears, while those that appeal to our other senses are accorded less dignity. Nevertheless, the senses of smell, taste, and touch have not been neglected. The emotional effects of different smells are poorly understood, though aromatherapists have developed some interesting taxonomies. The perfume industry is based on the emotional power of smell, and in many religions, from Buddhism to Christianity, worshippers burn incense to put themselves in a more contemplative mood.

The emotional effect of touch is better understood. Being caressed by another person releases natural opiates in the brain that are associated with a relaxed frame of mind. The evolutionary basis for this may lie in our recent primate past, around the time of the last

13 Humans have known about the emotional effects of smell for thousands of years. This Egyptian carving showing the priestess Ihat sniffing a lotus flower dates from around 2400 BC.

common ancestor of humans and chimpanzees, some five million years ago. Grooming may well have been as important for this creature as it is for modern chimpanzees, who spend hours each day removing the ticks from each other's fur. This grooming does not merely rid the other chimp of parasites; it also serves as a reliable sign of friendship. A preference for such a reliable signal of friendship would have motivated our furry ancestors to seek out friends. Those who did not like being groomed would have found themselves without allies when it came to a fight.

Just as our evolved visual preferences are the raw material for visual art, so our evolved tactile preferences are the raw material for massage. Massage is an old technology, like art and music. It was practised by the ancient Egyptians, and Hippocrates recommended doctors to 'be experienced in many things but assuredly in rubbing'. Today, orthodox medicine is beginning to rediscover the therapeutic value of massage, while it has been one of the central aspects of many alternative therapies for decades.

The gustatory technology of mood is, of course, cooking. By processing natural foods in a variety of ways, and combining them according to well-tested recipes, cooking does for natural flavours what painting does for natural colours and music for natural sounds. It cranks them up into a super-stimulus, tickling our taste buds more seductively than nature ever did. If strawberries taste good because they are sweet, cooks can make ultra-sugary things like strawberry ice cream that taste twice as good. Here, natural selection takes her revenge on us for daring to take the short cut to happiness instead of following the winding paths she set up for us to follow. Having given us a cheap and simple mechanism for finding glucose—a sweet tooth—she left us open to the dangers of wanting more than is good for us. In the stone age, that did not matter, since sugar came only in a rather diluted form called fruit. Today, however, where sugar comes in concentrated lumps called sweets, our intense desire for it can pose a serious problem for health. Obesity is now reaching epidemic levels in many affluent countries, and this is due largely to the dangerous combination of evolved desires for large amounts of sugar and fat, and the novel technology that is cooking.

Gustatory technologies of mood aim to induce good moods by stimulating our taste buds or by producing other chemical effects further downstream in the digestive process. Chocolate is quite an effective mood booster, as indeed are most foods and drinks that contain sugar. However, research has shown that, while most people feel more positive and energetic immediately after eating a chocolate bar, this effect soon wanes, and an hour afterwards they tend to feel even worse than they did before eating the chocolate in the first place. Tea and coffee have similar effects, with a short-term boost in mood being followed by a medium-term decrease. Most drugs have the same effect. In fact, the distinction between foodstuffs and drugs is a rather arbitrary one, and even today there is still no scientific basis for distinguishing drugs from the various other kinds of substance we consume. We tend to call something a drug if we consume it primarily for its psychotropic effects rather than for its nutritional or gustatory ones, but most kinds of food and drink have *some* effect on your state of mind. Cottage cheese and chicken liver, for example, both contain high levels of tryptophan, which the brain uses to make a chemical called serotonin, which in turn is associated with good moods. A friend of mine who is a vet once fed his dogs on a diet of cottage cheese and chicken liver for a week, after which they seemed much happier and more energetic than usual. Drugs are best seen as the end of a continuum of foods rather than a completely separate category.

The chemical route to happiness

Drugs are perhaps the most direct short cut to happiness. For those suffering from a severe case of depression, the chemical route to happiness may be the only one. Even so, many people feel reluctant to ask their doctor for antidepressants, even when nothing else seems to work for them. The same people might have no qualms about drinking a glass of wine, smoking a joint, or even taking a line of cocaine for recreational purposes, but when it comes to using mood-altering drugs for therapeutic purposes there is a curious aversion. Depression, they feel, is something that one must overcome on one's own. Using drugs to deal with it betrays some kind of moral weakness. The psychiatrist Gerald Klerman coined the term 'pharmacological Calvinism' to refer to this strange attitude to antidepressant drugs.

Whether mood-altering drugs are used for therapeutic purposes, as when a depressed patient is prescribed Prozac, or for recreational purposes, as when a party-goer takes Ecstasy, the chemical action is similar. Both Prozac and Ecstasy boost levels of serotonin. This has led some people to propose that serotonin is the chemical basis of mood. According to this theory, when there are high levels of serotonin in the brain, we are in a good mood, and when serotonin levels fall we get down. However, this simple hypothesis does not tally with all the evidence. Despite some claims that serotonin levels are depleted in the brains of suicidal patients, no abnormalities in the serotonin system have been consistently found in depressed people. Also, antidepressant drugs like Prozac boost serotonin levels in the brain as quickly as recreational drugs like Ecstasy— typically within an hour or two. Yet the antidepressant effects of Prozac are not usually felt as quickly as the euphoric effects of Ecstasy. Most depressed people have to take daily doses of Prozac for two or three weeks before they experience any alleviation of their symptoms, while the effects of Ecstasy are noticeable within forty-five minutes of taking a single dose. So moods cannot be just a question of serotonin levels in the brain. At present, despite the claims of various pharmaceutical companies, which have found that the seductive simplicity of the serotonin hypothesis makes it ideal for marketing their products, we simply do not know very much about the chemical details of mood or how antidepressant drugs work.

Other brain chemicals besides serotonin, such as dopamine and noradrenaline, also play an important part in mood. Drugs that affect these chemicals can, therefore, also be used to change one's emotional state.

Cocaine and amphetamines boost levels of dopamine and noradrenaline in the brain, and this is what seems to give them their euphoric properties. However, other drugs such as chlorpromazine, which boost levels of these chemicals almost as quickly as cocaine or amphetamine, do not produce the same instant euphoria, so once again the neural basis of mood must be more complicated than merely how much dopamine or noradrenaline you have sloshing around your grey matter.

As with chocolate, tea, and sugar, the mood-enhancing effects of most recreational drugs are short term, and the high may be followed by a distinctly unpleasant comedown. It is possible to maintain the high by taking another dose before the effects of the first wear off, but, the longer you stay up, the worse the eventual comedown. In an attempt to postpone the comedown indefinitely, some people become addicts, taking the drug continuously to maintain a permanent high. In such cases, maintaining the drug habit becomes the only valued activity in life, as everything else fades into insignificance. In an experiment conducted by James Olds, a rat was placed in a cage with a lever attached to a wire by means of which a current was applied to an electrode implanted in the reward centre of its brain. Every time the rat pressed the lever, the electrode stimulated a little burst of dopamine similar to the rush produced when a human snorts a line of cocaine. It was not long before the rat was spending all its time pressing the lever repeatedly, ignoring everything else around it, even food—a perfect image of the human drug addict.

As the addict's body and brain adapt to the drug, ever larger doses become necessary to achieve the same high. The long-term effects of pumping so much of the drug into the body are usually severe damage to various organs. Prolonged regular snorting of cocaine usually leads to sinusitis, nosebleeds, and a perforated nasal septum, and eventually heart attacks, strokes, and psychosis. Alcohol, one of the most addictive drugs, affects nearly every organ system, so alcoholics have increased rates of liver cirrhosis, stomach cancer, heart disease, and amnesia. With smoking, it is not the nicotine that poisons the body so much as the other components of the cigarette—tar and nitrogen dioxide—which cause heart disease, and lung cancer. The long-term effects of Ecstasy abuse are not yet known, although there are fears that it may increase the risk of depression and Alzheimer's disease.

Most drug-users manage to avoid these dangers by keeping their habit under control. Just as the majority of those who drink alcohol do not become alcoholics, so there are many people who use marijuana, Ecstasy, and cocaine without ever becoming addicted. Any drug, from tobacco and tea to cocaine and heroin, can be used responsibly if proper care is taken. Many respectable people used cocaine in the late nineteenth century, especially in the impure form that was an ingredient in the original Coca-Cola. Victorian gentlemen could often be seen smoking opium in the various dens around London. Sherlock Holmes injected morphine. The hysteria surrounding the use of such drugs today is largely a product of the current regulatory regime.

The simple fact is that no drug is without side effects. Even the most recent designer drugs have effects other than those for which they are prescribed. Besides alleviating depression, Prozac can increase anxiety, at least during the first few weeks of treatment. Taking Prozac can also make orgasm more difficult to achieve (although this is not always a bad thing). More subtle side effects of Prozac that have been reported include a sense of emotional numbness or distance, and lower sensitivity to the emotional needs of others. So, as a short cut to happiness, drugs are double-edged swords. Used wisely and responsibly, they can certainly brighten up one's life. On the other hand, the dangers of addiction (and, for certain drugs, the risk of arrest) threaten the unwary.

Like language, colour, and music, drugs are an ancient form of emotional technology. Alcohol may have been invented as recently as 5,000 or 6,000 years ago, but there is archaeological evidence that humans began using other psychotropic drugs long before this. The earliest use of these drugs seems to have been associated with religious ceremonies and other rituals, rather than the merely hedonistic purposes for which similar drugs are commonly used today. A thousand years ago, the Incas restricted the use of coca leaves, from which cocaine is derived, to the royal classes and the priesthood.

Whether a person takes a drug for hedonistic or spiritual purposes, the emotional effects of the drug are reasonably constant. The cavemen still got high on their sacred weeds. Indeed, if it were not for the emotional effects of these drugs, they would have been useless for religious purposes, as emotions are integral elements of religious experience. The same area of the brain that lights up in religious experience also lights up when people take LSD. Inducing the emotional state by taking drugs does not necessarily make it any less religious than inducing it by meditation or prayer. Conversely, 'religious' practices such as meditation may be used by atheists for the completely secular purpose of calming their mood.

Bodily technologies of mood

Meditation may be one of the safest technologies we have invented for regulating our emotional state. Eastern forms of meditation, which involve sitting still for long periods while emptying the mind and breathing regularly, are similar in many ways to the relaxation methods developed more recently in the West. Once again, the novel therapies of today turn out to be little more than scientific window dressing for practices that were first invented thousands of years ago.

In meditation and relaxation the calming effects are achieved by means of feedback from the body. The rhythmic breathing and the relaxed state of the muscles are interpreted by the brain as conducive to a calm frame of mind. Other moods can be induced by different kinds of bodily movement or posture. Going for a quick jog can induce a euphoric state of mind, and adopting certain facial expressions of emotion can lead you to feel the emotion itself. All these ways of inducing emotion could be referred to as bodily technologies of emotion.

As William James pointed out in 1882, the existence of such bodily technologies of emotion calls into question one of our common-sense beliefs about how emotions work. According to the common-sense view, emotions happen before bodily movements, and cause them. Bodily movements, such as sweating or smiling, are the expression of the emotion, not its cause. If we see a bear, for example, and run away, most of us would probably say that the sight of the bear causes us to feel afraid, and that this feeling then causes us to run. However, when meditation is used to induce a calm mood, or we go jogging to make ourselves feel happier, things are the other way round. In this case, it is the bodily movement that causes the emotion, not the emotion that causes the bodily movement.

James was pointing to the fact that the relationship between mind and body is not just one way. There is a feedback mechanism by which the body can affect the mind just as much as the mind affects the body. As with any feedback loop, this allows for amplification. James described the body as the mind's 'sounding board', allowing the emotional signal to resonate much as the soundbox of a guitar amplifies the sound of the strings. This is what explains our capacity for 'working ourselves up' into a florid emotional state, which James described with his customary eloquence:

Everyone knows how panic is induced by flight, and how giving way to the symptoms of grief increases those passions themselves. Each fit of sobbing makes the sorrow more acute, and calls forth another fit stronger still, until at last repose ensues only with lassitude and with the apparent exhaustion of the machinery.

Conversely, as the bodily technologies of emotion make clear, the feedback mechanism also allows us to exercise some measure of control over our emotions by deliberately suppressing some automatic bodily changes and consciously making others. If crying makes the sorrow more acute, then fighting back the tears should make the emotion less intense. In James's words:

If we wish to conquer undesirable emotional tendencies in ourselves, we must assiduously, and in the first instance cold-bloodedly, go through the outward motions of those contrary dispositions we prefer to cultivate. . . . Smooth the brow, brighten the eye, contract the dorsal rather than the ventral aspect of the frame, and speak in a major key, pass the genial compliment, and your heart must be frigid indeed if it does not gradually thaw!

There is some evidence that this strategy works. Paul Ekman, the anthropologist whose work on facial expressions I discussed in Chapter One, came across this bodily technology of emotion by accident, while he was developing a technique for measuring the movement of facial muscles. While contracting the muscles associated with typical facial expressions of emotion, Ekman and his colleague Wallace Friesen found themselves experiencing strong emotional sensations. In a follow-up experiment, they gave subjects muscle-by-muscle instructions to produce facial configurations for various basic emotions, without telling the subjects that these voluntary movements would lead them to adopt the facial expressions associated with various emotions. The subjects were then asked if they had experienced any feelings. The feelings reported by the subjects were almost always those associated with the particular facial expressions that they had unwittingly adopted.

Of course, there are limits. You cannot make yourself a lot happier simply by adopting a forced smile, despite what some self-help books may tell you. This is because many muscles involved in emotional expression are beyond voluntary control. When you smile spontaneously, for example, the *orbicularis oculi* (the muscle that encircles each eye) contracts on both sides, raising the cheeks and gathering the skin inwards towards the nose. This muscle is not easily brought under voluntary control, which is why it is usually quite easy to tell a genuine smile from a fake one. Simply curving your lips upward at each end does not produce a complete expression of joy, so doing this will not induce much joy either.

The distinction between muscles that are under voluntary control and those that are not is not a hard and fast one, however. By using techniques such as yoga or biofeedback, people can be trained to gain some measure of conscious control over autonomic functions that are normally involuntary. Perhaps if we could gain even greater voluntary control over our bodies, the bodily technologies of emotion would not only be safer than the other technologies mentioned here: they might also be more effective.

Many bodily technologies of mood do not just produce short-term benefits for mood; they also brighten our outlook on life in the long term. Going for a short run may lead to a brief buzz, but doing so every day will also boost your overall health, which is one of the best predictors of general life satisfaction. Sports in general can be seen as providing a variety of bodily technologies of mood, as can dance, which has similar mood-boosting powers. Unlike drugs, which tend to boost short-term happiness at the expense of decreasing long-term happiness, the bodily technologies of emotion are good for you in both the short term and the long term.

Sports and dance do not simply increase the happiness of those who take part. When done with grace and skill, they also increase the happiness of the spectator. It is not hard to see why this should be the case. Those of our ancestors who derived pleasure from observing agility would have been more likely to associate with and perhaps have sex with agile people. They would have had fitter offspring than those who preferred to associate with the stone-age equivalent of couch potatoes. Spectator sports and performance art are the technologies that play on our innate preferences for observing skill and agility, just as painting plays on our innate preferences for observing certain colours and forms.

In choosing our short cuts to happiness, we are not necessarily faced with a stark alternative between the various technologies of mood. We can pick and mix, combining them in accordance with our tastes and values. The mixing of different art forms was held in high esteem by the Romantics, who coined the term 'synaesthesia' for such combinations. Opera was a prime example of synaesthesia, combining drama, poetry, music, song, dance, and painting to produce a cornucopia of sensory delights. Films, musicals, and video games can be seen as modern forms of synaesthesia. The most intense combination of pleasures, however, may well be the rave.

In these events, the whole gamut of technologies of

14 Raves: are they the ultimate short cut to happiness?

emotion—linguistic, sensory, chemical, and bodily— are combined to produce an extremely intense form of happiness. Coloured lights swirl around, delighting the eyes. Rhythmic music stirs the heart. Ecstasy pills unleash cascades of serotonin in the brain and smart-drinks give tiny caffeine boosts. Wild dancing induces a trancelike state. If someone has a bad trip, soft words are used to calm him down. Aching muscles may be relieved by a holistic massage from one of the alternative therapists who sometimes hang around the more spiritual raves. Once again, though, this combination of emotional technologies is hardly new. Since the dawn of humanity, people have regularly come together to dance and take drugs. The party may well be the ultimate short cut to happiness.

4

The head and the heart

Basic emotions are not always present, and most if not all higher cognitive emotions are fairly transient states too. For much, perhaps most, of the time, we are not in the grip of fear, nor swooning with love. In this neutral frame of mind, we can usually think quite logically. We are clear-headed and can spot bad arguments relatively easily. Things are quite different, however, when a strong emotion wells up in us, or a powerful mood takes us over. At these times the head becomes a slave to the heart.

People have long been interested in the way that emotions affect our cognitive capacities. In his book on rhetoric, Aristotle noted that 'feelings are conditions that cause us to change and alter our judgements'. In recent years, a growing amount of experimental work has helped to pinpoint the nature of these effects. This chapter explores some of this work in relation to three cognitive capacities: attention, memory, and logical reasoning.

The mental spotlight

Attention is the name that psychologists give to our capacity to focus on a particular thought or activity. It is rather like a spotlight in the head that can be pointed at different mental activities. Even though there might be hundreds of things going on in our minds, we can train our mental spotlight on only a few of them at any one moment. When we are concentrating hard on something like a crossword puzzle or a difficult sum, other thoughts cannot be entertained. If we are suddenly disturbed by a loud noise, fear points the spotlight at the new event.

Spotlights can be more or less focused. When focused to their maximum extent, they illuminate a very small area with a very bright light. When de-focused, they illuminate a larger area, but the light is less intense. The same is true for attention. When we are relaxed, and not in the grip of any particular emotion, our mental spotlight is relatively unfocused, and more thoughts may drift through our awareness. When an emotion occurs, however, our mental spotlight suddenly contracts, focusing on one small thought to the exclusion of all others. This thought is usually a representation of the external object that caused the emotion. When we are afraid, for example, the mental spotlight focuses on the thing that frightened us. Anger makes us dwell on the thing that annoyed us. Love makes it hard to think of anything except the beloved. Emotions are often blamed for distracting us, so it might seem strange to say that they help to focus our attention. There is, however, no contradiction; emotions distract us from one thought only in order to make us pay attention to another.

Attention is affected by moods too. Moods, you will recall, are different from emotions. They typically last much longer than basic emotions, working in the background by raising or lowering our susceptibility to emotional stimuli. Like emotions, however, moods force the mental spotlight to contract, though probably not as much as emotions do (happiness may be an exception to this rule, enlarging our attention, making the spotlight more diffuse). People in an anxious mood tend to be preoccupied by thoughts of their own safety, but, unlike someone in a state of fright, they are able to think about a few other things too.

Like emotions, moods tend to make us focus on thoughts about the things that caused the mood. When we are in an irritable mood, we may brood about the things that have recently annoyed us. Sometimes, however, a mood may overtake us without focusing our attention on anything in particular. We may become anxious without being aware of the cause of our anxiety. Such 'free-floating' anxiety still affects attention, however. Instead of forcing us to focus on a particular thought, it clears thoughts away, prompting us to attend to the world around us. If we walk down a dark alley late at night, an anxious mood leads us to scan the shadows for signs of movement.

In this situation, anxiety is clearly a useful thing. A person in an anxious mood is on the lookout for possible threats, and is therefore able to respond more quickly should anything untoward actually occur. The threats need not be physical. Anything that might prevent you from achieving a goal can be seen as a threat. If your goal is to give a good speech at your best friend's wedding, the biggest threat might be your tendency to stutter when nervous. An anxious mood would then prompt you to be on the lookout for the tiniest hint of hesitation in your speech. Should you notice such hesitation, of course, this will only make you more anxious, and you may find yourself degenerating into a nervous stammer. On such occasions, anxiety becomes counterproductive.

Psychologists have investigated the effects of anxiety on attention by means of an experiment known as the 'emotional Stroop test'. The original Stroop test has nothing to do with emotion. It involves showing people words printed in different coloured inks, and asking them to say what the colour of the ink was. The time between the moment when the word appears on the screen, and the moment when the person gives the right answer, is carefully measured. The trick is that some of the words are also the names of colours, and sometimes the colour of the ink in which these words are printed is different from the colour named by the word. When this happens, it is mildly confusing, so that reaction times are slower. People are quicker at saying what the colour of the ink is when it matches the colour named by the word—when the word 'red' is printed in red ink, for example—than when it does not.

The emotional version of the Stroop test uses words with strong emotional connotations rather than the names of colours, but, like the original Stroop test, the words are still printed in different coloured inks, and people are asked to say what the colour of the ink is. When people are shown a word with strong emotional connotations, they typically take longer to say what the colour of the ink is than when the word is emotionally neutral. Of course, different words carry different emotional connotations for different people. Words connected with rape, for example, will be more emotionally charged for rape victims than for others. This shows up in the emotional Stroop test too. One study found that, compared to other people, rape victims were much slower at saying what the colour of the ink was when the words were related to rape. It appears that the anxiety generated by seeing a word connected with a traumatic experience focuses the attention on the meaning of the word, making it harder to pay attention to peripheral details like the colour of the ink in which the word is printed.

Emotion and memory

Besides affecting attention, emotions and moods also play an important part in memory. Like attention, memory is highly selective. We remember only a tiny amount of the things we experience. Memory space is limited, so we have to use it economically, storing as little as possible and forgetting as soon as is expedient. Anything else would make life impossible, as is clear from a story by the Argentinian writer Jorge Luis Borges. In 'Funes the Memorious', a boy called Ireneo becomes paralysed after being thrown from his horse. But the accident also has a strange effect on his mind: it makes his memory infallible. From then on, he remembers every single sight and sound in perfect detail. Needless to say, this makes his life a misery (see Box below).

Funes—the man with the perfect memory

He knew by heart the forms of the southern clouds at dawn on 30 April 1882, and could compare them in his memory with the mottled streaks on a book in Spanish binding he had seen only once, and with the outlines of the foam raised by an oar in the Río Negro the night before the Quebracho uprising. These memories were not simple ones; each visual image was linked to muscular sensations, thermal sensations, etc. He could reconstruct all his dreams, all his half-dreams. Two or three times he had reconstructed a whole day; he never hesitated, but each reconstruction had required another whole day. He told me: 'I alone have more memories than all mankind has probably had since the world has been the world.' . . . .

I suspect, however, that he was not very capable of thought. To think is to forget differences, generalise, make abstractions. In the teeming world of Funes, there were only details, almost immediate in their presence.

Source: Jorge Luis Borges,
'Funes the Memorious' (1956)

When something is stored in the memory, then, it is not recorded in all its finest detail, but rather filed away under a few keywords. When we come to recall something from memory, we extract some of these keywords, and fill in the rest by educated guesswork. Remembering is, therefore, never exact. It is more like reconstructing an antique pot from a few broken shards than replaying an old movie. Some memories seem so fresh and vivid when we recall them that we may have the impression of reliving the event exactly as it happened, but this is an illusion caused by the power of our imaginative reconstruction. When we compare such recollections with those of others who were in the same place at the same time, we may find that the accounts differ markedly, while the differing versions seem equally vivid and real to each person.

In *Chronicle of a Death Foretold*, by Gabriel Garcia Márquez, a man returns to a village where, years before, a violent murder had occurred. Talking to the villagers, the man discovers that almost all of them have some recollection of the murder. However, everyone remembers the murder differently. All the villagers stored the event in their memory under different keywords, and, in recalling the event, they all fill in the gaps by drawing on the unique resources of their own imaginations. Naturally, the friends and family of the victim recall the murder differently from the man's more distant acquaintances and his enemies. Emotions clearly play an important part in memory, both in the way we store something in our memory, and in the way we reconstruct it when we recall it.

The ease and accuracy with which we recall an event are affected by both the emotional state we were in when the event occurred and the mood we are in when we recall it. Freud thought that memories of negatively charged emotional events would be 'repressed' and therefore harder to recall, but in fact precisely the opposite is the case. Traumatic memories do not retreat into some dark recess of the mind, as Freud supposed. Rather, they obtrude persistently into consciousness, perturbing us when we would rather forget them, even disrupting our dreams. In severe cases, this is known as 'post-traumatic stress disorder', a syndrome character-ized by vivid flashbacks in which the person relives the event in painful detail.

Emotions help to etch events more deeply in our memories. Any event that produces a strong emotion in us, whether negative or positive, is recalled more easily and more accurately than an emotionally neutral event. In one study, three groups of students were shown a set of fifteen slides, each of which showed a sight that you might see while walking to work. Each group saw the same set of slides, except for slide number eight, of which there were three different versions (see Fig. 15).

In one, a woman was riding a bicycle. In another, the same woman was carrying the bicycle on her shoulder. In the third version, the woman was lying by the roadside with the bicycle lying next to her, as if she had been knocked down by a car. When asked to recall what they had seen, the group who had been shown the slide with the woman lying on the ground remembered the colour of her coat much better than the other groups, but they were much worse at recalling peripheral details such as the colour of a car in the distance. This suggests that the core features of emotionally charged events are remembered better than those of neutral events; the peripheral features, however, fade away more quickly.

The ease and accuracy of recall are also influenced by the mood we are in when we remember something. Dozens of experiments conducted by the psychologist Gordon Bower show that, when we are in a happy mood, we tend to recall pleasant events more easily and more accurately than unpleasant ones. The opposite is true when we are in a sad mood. This phenomenon is known as 'mood-congruent recall'. In one experiment, Bower asked people to recall incidents of any kind from their childhood, and to describe each one. The next day, when the same people were in a neutral mood, he

15 The three versions of the critical eighth slide in the experiment described on pp. 120–121.

asked them to label each incident as pleasant, unpleasant, or neutral. The following day, a happy or a sad mood was artificially induced in each person by means of hypnotic suggestion, and they were then asked to recall as many of the incidents as they could. Bower found that those in a good mood remembered many of the incidents they had labelled as pleasant, but few of those they had labelled as unpleasant. Those in a bad mood, on the other hand, remembered more of the unpleasant incidents.

A possible explanation for the phenomenon of mood-congruent recall is that, when events are stored in the memory, they are tagged with an emotional marker indicating which emotion, if any, was present when the event was experienced. When we recall events from memory, those that are tagged with a marker that is compatible with the current emotional state are given more salience. Keith Oatley and Jennifer Jenkins have suggested that this may help us to deal with a current situation more easily by bringing to mind incidents comparable to the one that provoked the current mood.

Judging people and evaluating arguments

In addition to their effects on attention and memory, emotions and moods also exert a powerful influence on decision-making and judgement. For example, the opinions we form of other people are often affected by the mood we happen to be in when we meet them. People in a good mood are likely to judge the same person more positively than people in a bad mood. In one experiment, good and bad moods were induced artificially by telling people that they had done very well or very badly in a mock test. They were then asked to interview someone by asking them a prearranged set of questions, such as 'What are your most important traits'. Unbeknownst to the students, the people they were interviewing were in league with the experimenters, and all gave exactly the same answers to the questions. The answers were deliberately ambiguous, revealing both positive things ('I'm pretty friendly') and negative things ('I'm quite stubborn and impatient') about the interviewee. Afterwards, the interviewers were asked to evaluate the interviewee on personal and professional grounds. Sure enough, the interviewers who had been put in a good mood tended to rate the interviewees more positively than those who had been put in a bad mood, even though the answers they received were the same. Those in a good mood were also more likely to say that they would hire the interviewee for a job.

It is not just happy and sad moods that influence our judgements of other people. Anxiety can also affect the way we see others. The precise way in which it affects such judgements, however, is quite surprising. Rather than making us view strangers in a negative way, being in an anxious mood can actually make us feel closer to them. This, at least, seems to be the conclusion of one famous experiment conducted in the 1970s. Men crossing a high, rather scary suspension bridge were stopped by a young woman, who asked them if they would take part in a survey. She then gave them a card with her phone number on, saying that she would be happy to talk to them about the survey in greater detail if they wanted. Later the same day, she did the same thing on a much lower and safer bridge. During the following days, many more phone calls were received from the men who had met the woman on the scary bridge than from those who had met her on the safe one. The anxiety seems to have made them more friendly, perhaps even flirtatious.

This bonding effect of anxiety may perhaps provide part of the explanation for the strange phenomenon of hostages coming to care deeply about their captors.

Some of this may simply be due to the close proximity in which hostages and captors live during their brief relationships, but even so it seems likely that such affection for one's captor is intensified by the anxiety that lurks constantly in the mind of the hostage. The well-known story of how British and German soldiers left their trenches on Christmas Day in 1914 to play football with each other may be apocryphal, but it too points to the same bonding effect of anxiety. This conjunction of anxiety and affection seems counter-intuitive, but perhaps there is some logic to it. Maybe it evolved to help our ancestors join forces in dangerous situations, when there was safety in numbers.

As well as affecting the way we judge other people, moods also influence our susceptibility to weak arguments. Here, though, it is not just a question of what mood one happens to be in when listening to the argument, but also of how much time one has to think about it. When people are in a neutral mood, or have lots of time to think, bad arguments are not very persuasive. But when they are in a good mood and have little time to think, people are more influenced by invalid arguments (and less by valid ones). It seems that the combination of being in a good mood and being in a rush forces one to take short cuts, basing one's judgement less on logical analysis and more on contextual clues such as the reputation of the speaker.

To test this idea, Diane Mackie and Leila Worth quizzed American students to see whether or not they were in favour of greater gun control. A positive mood was then induced in half of the students by showing them a five-minute extract from a comedy programme. The others watched an emotionally neutral extract from a programme about wine. Each group was then presented with an argument advancing a view about gun control that ran contrary to their own opinions. Those who were in favour of greater gun control read an argument opposing such restrictions, while those against gun control read an argument in favour. Half were presented with weak arguments and half with strong logical arguments. Some of the students were told that the person presenting the argument was an expert, while others were told that they were reading the views of a first-year student. Furthermore, some were given a short time to read the argument, while others were allowed to take as long as they wanted. After reading the argument, the students were re-tested to see if their views on gun control had changed.

Overall, everyone was more influenced by the good arguments than by the bad ones. But, for those in a positive mood with little time to think, the difference was very small. Whereas all the other groups found the weak arguments much less persuasive, those in a good mood and in a rush found the bad arguments almost as persuasive as the good ones. Further testing revealed that this group had given much more weight to the reputation of the speaker when reading the argument. The fact that the happy people who were allowed to take as long as they wanted found the weak arguments as unpersuasive as those in a bad mood might seem to point to time being the crucial variable rather than mood. However, when Mackie and Worth compared the actual time taken by the two groups who were allowed to examine the arguments as long as they wanted, they found that those in a good mood actually took *longer* than those in a bad mood. They inferred from this that being in a good mood makes you more easily swayed by bad arguments, but that most people seem to be aware of this fact at some level, and so automatically compensate for this by taking longer to think about things when their critical powers are blunted by happiness! (See Fig. 16)

The research of Mackie and Worth suggests that there are two ways of forming judgements about complex issues. One way is slow but very precise. The other is quick and dirty. The slow but precise way relies mainly on logic, but the quick and dirty way relies heavily on

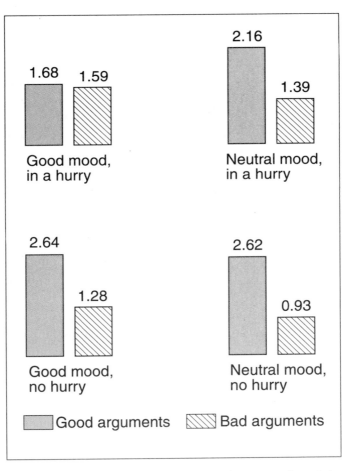

16 Graph showing results of the experiment conducted by Diane Mackie and Leila Worth. People in a good mood and in a hurry found bad arguments almost as persuasive as good ones. All other groups found weak arguments much less persuasive. The height of the bars and the figures indicate how persuasive each group found each type of argument (the higher the bar and the figure, the more persuasive the group found the argument).

emotion. Reason and emotion can thus be seen as two complementary systems in the human brain for making decisions. When it is important to get the answer right, and we have a lot of time and information at our disposal, we can use the slow and clean method of reasoning things through. When we have little time and information, or it is not so important to get the right answer, we can switch to the fast and frugal method of following our feelings.

Sometimes, however, we use the wrong system. On the one hand, we may overestimate the amount of time and information we have at our disposal or the importance of getting the decision right, and then end up reasoning about something when we would have been better off consulting our feelings. The neuroscientist Antonio Damasio tells a story about a brain-damaged patient of his who could not help overusing the rational system. After a check-up, Damasio asked the patient when he would like to come for his next appointment. When Damasio suggested two possible dates, just a few days apart, the patient pulled out his diary and began to list the advantages and disadvantages of attending on each. For almost half an hour, he weighed up the possible weather conditions on each day, the need to cancel other engagements, and dozens of other relevant factors. Damasio listened to all this with great patience, before finally suggesting, quietly, that the patient should come on the second of the two dates. 'OK', smiled the patient, snapping shut his diary as if nothing odd had happened.

As this story illustrates, when there is not much at stake in making a decision, we are better off saving time by using the quick and dirty emotional system rather than the slower rational one. On the other hand, there are times when it is so important to arrive at the right judgement that considerations of time are better left aside. For example, when we want to find out whether or not someone is guilty of murder, or how fast light travels through a vacuum, getting the right the answer is so important that we are prepared to sacrifice time for accuracy. In these cases, the impact of emotions on decision-making can be positively harmful, and we seek ways of diminishing their influence.

Are two heads really better than one?

It is widely supposed that one way to do this is to institutionalize the decision-making process, transforming it from an individual action into a collective one. The hope is that, in the communal debate, the emotional biases of individuals will cancel each other out, leaving pure reason to emerge as the exclusive basis for judgement. Two heads are supposed to be better than one, because they are supposed to be less emotional. In science, the peer review process is supposed to filter out the rival emotions of various disputants, so that they may reach agreement by purely rational means. In the legal system of most countries today, decisions about important cases are taken not by a single judge but by a jury of twelve. Once again, the hope is that twelve heads will be better than one, because their conflicting emotions will cancel each other out, leaving pure reason to be the final arbiter.

Unfortunately, there are reasons to doubt this rosy view of institutional decision-making. For a start, a lack of time is not the only indication for making decisions by gut feeling. Even when there is plenty of time, some very important decisions should still be based on emotion. Getting married is one. When Darwin was deciding whether or not to marry, he marked two columns on a piece of paper, listing the advantages of marriage in one and the advantages of bachelorhood in the other, and then observed which had more. The method seemed to work: Darwin went on to marry his cousin, Emma Wedgwood, and by all accounts it was a very happy union. Most people, however, would probably think this an overly rational way to make a decision about affairs of the heart. Even Darwin was not being entirely rational, however. In attaching different weights to each point he noted, he must have consulted his feelings, for there is still no scientific way of calculating the utility of a preference.

Deciding whether or not to trust someone is also better done by consulting one's feelings than by reasoning. Those who lose part of their emotional capacity through brain damage of one kind or another tend to be easy victims for the unscrupulous. Forced to rely entirely on their logical reasoning, they make disastrous choices about whom they can trust. Most normal people, on the other hand, are very good at telling who is trustworthy from who is not. By some half-conscious, intuitive means, most of us are very good at sussing people out. This ability is lacking in people who have suffered damage to their amygdala. As we saw in Chapter Two, this is one of the key brain regions involved in emotion, so it is probable that our intuitive capacity for sussing people out is mediated largely by emotional processes.

When we speak of emotions affecting rational decision-making, then, we should not regard this as an inherently bad thing. It may be of benefit to base our decisions on emotional factors in more situations than we realize. If science *does* progress better because of its collectivization of decision-making, and if justice *is* served better by juries than by individual judges, this may be because the collective is *more* emotional than the individual, not less. Perhaps the jury is better at sussing out the defendant than the lone judge because twelve *hearts* are better than one.

Psychologists have long been aware of the power of social groups to amplify emotions, but they have tended to view this with suspicion rather than admiration. Writing at the end of the nineteenth century, the French psychologist Gustave LeBon described in chilling terms how people can be swept away by the passions of the crowd, working themselves up into a frenzy more vicious than anything of which they would be capable on their own. More recently, psychologists have speculated that demagogues such as Hitler and Mussolini achieved and maintained their power in part by taking advantage of a primitive 'group mind', in which collective emotion drowns out the individual voice of reason. Collective emotion can be a powerful force, but most intellectuals, fearful of the uneducated masses, have regarded this power as dangerous rather than as liberating. Karl Marx is a notable exception.

For good or ill, and perhaps both, the tendency for emotion to be amplified in social groups begs for explanation. Are we programmed to be conformists, secretly fascinated by the power of authority, as the psychologists of the Frankfurt School wondered darkly in the aftermath of the Second World War? Or is there a deeper biological reason for the power of emotional contagion?

Some evolutionary psychologists have suggested that our susceptibility to group influence provided a useful guide to action when our ancestors were less able to work things out for themselves. If in doubt about what course of action to take, doing what the others are doing might well be the best solution. At the very least, your errors will not lead others to ridicule you, because they will have made the same mistakes. Innovation is a risky strategy. When it works, others admire you. But when it does not, you look like a fool.

Sympathy and suggestion

Whatever the reason for the 'herd mentality' that can overtake us when we are in tightly knit social groups, it seems to rest on our capacity for sympathy. Sympathy means feeling someone else's emotions as if they were your own. Some people prefer to call this empathy, and reserve the term 'sympathy' for a less intense form of sharing someone else's feelings in which some critical

17 Hitler addresses two million people on May Day, 1934. Like many other demagogues, Hitler knew that collective emotion can drown out the individual voice of reason.

distance is maintained. Terminology aside, it is clear that the capacity of social groups to amplify emotion could not exist were it not for the individual ability to take on board someone else's emotion and feel it in one's own heart.

Adam Smith regarded sympathy as one of the highest virtues, and dedicated the first part of his first book, *The Theory of Moral Sentiments*, to exploring it. The same appreciation of the capacity for sympathy and empathy underlies the current vogue for emotional intelligence. Sympathy is not without its dark side too, however. By laying us open to the emotional influence of others, sympathy gives them an extra way of inducing emotions in us for the purposes of persuasion. As the research on the emotional influences on judgement shows, appealing to people's emotions may offer a more direct way of changing their mind than rational argument.

By the third century BC, the Ancient Greeks had already accumulated a large body of technique and theory concerning the use of emotions in persuasion. Today, advertisers use similar techniques to get us to buy particular products. They may use humour to put us in a good mood, hoping that this will render us more vulnerable to their otherwise unpersuasive arguments. Or they may try to make us afraid of what might happen if we do not buy their products. In one of Saki's short stories, sales of a disgusting breakfast cereal rocket after a clever advertising campaign. Posters display sombre images of the damned in hell suffering a new torment from their inability to get at the cereal, which elegant young fiends hold in transparent bowls just beyond their reach. Underneath the picture, a single grim statement runs in bold letters: 'They cannot buy it now.'

One technique of persuasion that relies on the power of emotion to influence our judgements is subliminal advertising. Contrary to what many people imagine, most subliminal advertising is not all about flashing phrases such as 'Buy this product' or 'Vote for me' across your TV screen too quickly for you to process them consciously. There are many other forms of subliminal advertising that are much less sneaky. 'Sub-liminal' just means that something enters your mind without you noticing it; it enters by means of a secret passage beneath the threshold of consciousness (*limen* is Latin for 'threshold'). This happens all the time without the need for fancy technology. When you walk past a billboard, most of the time you do not stop to read the blurb. You may not even notice it consciously. But the image may have been processed by some bit of your brain without you knowing. A massive advertising campaign need not worry if its slogans are devoid of logical argument; the sense of familiarity with the product that is produced by sensory bombardment will do the trick by itself.

Familiarity does not, it seems, always breed contempt. On the contrary, what is already known can bring a sense of reassurance. The known is inherently less threatening than the perils of the unknown. It was not a fear of death that led Hamlet to reject suicide, but the possibility of unknown agonies beyond the grave. More prosaically, the preference for what is known underlies the pleasures of nostalgic reminiscence and the company of old friends. Like most emotional phenomena, this inherent conservatism has its downside too. When it is combined with a strong sense of group identity, it can lead to all sorts of prejudice, from racism and xenophobia to ethnocentrism and religious bigotry.

The universal preference for the familiar is known in psychology as 'the mere-exposure effect'. The term was coined by Robert Zajonc, whose work in the late 1970s and early 1980s helped to bring emotions back into the mainstream of cognitive science. Zajonc demonstrated the effect in a series of ingenious experiments. In order to show that preferences could be formed on the basis of familiarity alone—on the basis of mere *exposure*—he flashed some visual patterns on a screen so quickly that the viewers did not notice them consciously. In sorting through a group of patterns afterwards, the subjects of the experiment were unable to identify which ones they had seen before. If, however, they were asked which ones they preferred, they picked out exactly those they had been shown earlier. *Some* bit of their brain must have processed the image, even though they were unaware of it.

The funniest thing about this experiment was that if people were asked to say why they preferred the patterns they did, they gave a whole range of reasons. Perhaps one symbol had a particularly elegant symmetry. Another might suggest a picture of a smiling face. But these could not be the real explanation, because other people said very similar things about completely different patterns. The only thing in common between the patterns that people preferred was the fact that they had been perceived before, though not consciously.

If something has been perceived subliminally, it is stored in a part of the memory that is inaccessible to conscious recall. It can, however, be accessed by an unconscious form of recall, as Zajonc's experiments with the mere-exposure effect show. This unconscious form of remembering usually manifests itself to consciousness as a feeling. If the subliminal memory has not been tagged with a particular emotion—if the event that occasioned it was perceived while in an emotionally neutral state—then the unconscious recall system will regard the memory in a positive light. This is what Zajonc's experiments suggest, anyway. The subjects of the experiment did not perceive the visual patterns while in a particularly good mood. Subliminal perception while in a neutral mood was sufficient to create a favourable response. Presumably, the mere-exposure effect works for other things too, such as familiar music and familiar food. Human beings are creatures of habit.

If, however, the subliminal memory is tagged with a negative emotion, things are different. Things perceived unconsciously while in a state of fear, for example, may be stored in the unconscious memory with a negative tag. Later, when we encounter the same object, we may experience a curious aversion that we cannot explain. A gut feeling tells us to avoid the object, even though we do not know why (see Box below). This can have undesirable consequences, such as a disabling phobia, but it can also stop us from making silly mistakes.

Sometimes nature carries out an experiment that it would be cruel for humans to perform, and removes the conscious recall system through disease or accident. Total amnesia may also result from a medical operation that goes wrong. Whatever the cause, amnesia usually leaves the unconscious recall system intact, allowing us

Subliminal reactions to emotional faces

In 1998, the Irish neuroscientist Ray Dolan, together with colleagues John Morris and Arne Öhman, found that the brain processes facial expressions of emotion at an unconscious as well as at a conscious level. In one experiment, they showed two slides of angry faces to people. While one of the slides was shown, a burst of unpleasant 'white noise' was played, thus ensuring that the memory of this face would have a negative affective marker attached to it. The other angry face was presented without any accompanying sound.

In the next part of the experiment, one of the slides was flashed up very quickly, immediately followed by a slide of an expressionless face. This is called 'backward masking', because perception of the second slide masks the perception of the first. When asked what they saw, subjects reported seeing the second slide, but not the first.

Even though they did not report seeing the first slide, the subjects must have perceived it at some unconscious level, because their brain activity was different depending on whether the first slide was the one that was associated with the unpleasant noise or not. In other words, the first slide had been perceived *subliminally*. The main brain region associated with the unconscious recognition of the negatively charged face was the right amygdala. Once again, the amygdala had turned out to play a crucial role in unconscious emotional processing. Whenever you have a gut reaction to someone you have never met—whenever, that is, you 'just don't like the look of someone'—it is probably because your amygdala is telling you that the stranger looks like someone who has done something bad to you, even though you don't have any conscious recall of the old foe.

Source: J. S. Morris, A. Öhman, and R. J. Dolan, 'Conscious and Unconscious Emotional Learning in the Human Amygdala', *Nature*, 393/6684 (1998), 467–70

to see it unhindered by the glare of conscious recall. One famous amnesiac could not commit anything new to conscious memory from the time of her accident, so, for example, she never recognized her doctor, even though she saw him every day. One day the doctor entered the patient's room with a sharp pin secretly attached to his palm. On shaking the doctor's hand, the patient received a mild pinprick, and withdrew her hand abruptly. The next day, the patient greeted the doctor as if he were a complete stranger, just as usual, but this time she refused to shake the doctor's outstretched hand. Like the subjects in Zajonc's experiments, the woman was unable to say *why* she would not shake the doctor's hand. She just didn't feel like it. An unconscious memory was able to manifest itself as an emotion, even after her conscious recall system had been destroyed.

The head, it seems, is not always master of the heart. Nor, as we have seen, is this a bad thing. The emotions inform our decisions even when we think we are being completely rational. However, the heart is not completely in control either. Contrary to Hume's famous remark, reason is not always passion's slave. Sometimes our heads are empty of emotion, and it is then that we may do some of our finest analytical work. Ideally, however, we are neither completely rational nor completely emotional, but manage to strike the elegant balance between the two that we refer to as emotional intelligence.

The computer that cried

The idea that machines might one day come to have emotions is a recurrent theme in science-fiction movies. In *2001: A Space Odyssey*, HAL—the onboard computer who turns against the crew of the spaceship *Discovery 1*—utters cries of pain and fear when his circuits are finally taken apart. In *Blade Runner*, a humanoid robot is distressed to learn that her memories are not real, but have been implanted in her silicon brain by her programmer. In *Bicentennial Man*, Robin Williams plays the part of a robot who redesigns his own circuitry so that it will allow him to experience the full range of human emotion.

These stories achieve their effect in part because the capacity for emotion is often considered to be one of the main differences between humans and machines. This is certainly true of the machines we know today. The responses we receive from computers are rather dry affairs, such as 'System error 1378'. This is a long

18 HAL, the onboard computer in *2001: A Space Odyssey*.

way from the agonizing screams of HAL. People some-times get angry with their computers and shout at them as if they had emotions, but the computers take no notice. They neither feel their own feelings, nor recognize yours.

The gap between science fiction and science fact appears vast, but some researchers in artificial intelligence now believe it is only a question of time before it is bridged. The new field of affective computing has already made some progress in building primitive emotional machines, and every month brings new advances. However, some critics argue that a machine could never come to have real emotions like ours. At best, they claim, clever programming might allow it to *simulate* human emotions, but these would just be clever fakes. Who is right? To answer this question, we need to say what emotions really *are*.

It might appear rather odd that it is only now, in the final chapter, that I have got round to defining emotion. Most introductory books *start* with a definition, but I prefer to leave such things to the end, where they can do less damage. Definitions are useful for resolving disputes, but they can easily become intellectual straitjackets, tempting people into the mistaken belief that words have fixed or essential meanings that should be defended against the tide of cultural change and scientific progress. A brief discussion of what emotions 'really are' may help us to decide when a computer could be said to have emotions, but the definition(s) we hit on should be regarded as provisional and always open to revision.

There are several ways we might go about constructing a definition of emotion. One way would be to start with the neurobiological details. Another would be to define emotion in behavioural terms. A third might use functional criteria, by defining emotions in terms of their role in the mental economy. Finally, we might take subjective feelings to be the essence of emotion. This last way seems to be the most common view, at least among the general public.

All of these criteria refer to widely acknowledged features of emotion, but most contemporary philosophers and psychologists who write about emotion reject any simple definition of emotion in terms of a single criterion. Rather, there is now a consensus that emotions comprise a number of related processes, and that it is pointless to single out any one of these as the 'essence' of emotional phenomena. This applies to feelings just as much as to any other aspect of emotion. There is no more justification for regarding feelings as the sine qua non of emotion than there is for any other aspect, such as facial expression or the narrowing of attention. Normally, all the aspects of emotion are combined in a single emotional event. When one of them is not present, such as when a person feels an emotion but does not make the relevant facial expression, we are not immediately inclined to deny that an emotion has occurred. It would be equally senseless to deny that a computer did not have true emotions just because it happened to lack one element of emotion, such as conscious feelings, but possessed all the others.

I will return to the subject of feelings at the end of the chapter. First, however, let us look at neurobiological, behavioural, and functional definitions of emotion, and see how computers might fare on these grounds. Defining emotions in neurobiological terms is relatively straightforward. Now that we know, for example, that basic emotions are mediated largely by the limbic system, we might go on to define emotion as a limbic brain process. By this definition, computers could never be said to have emotions, because they do not have limbic systems. Nor could intelligent aliens ever be said to have emotions, unless their brains also happened to be structured in very similar ways to ours. This, however, is a rather parochial view of emotion. To say that an alien was incapable of emotion just because it lacked a few bizarrely shaped neural structures that we have inherited from our furry ancestors seems arbitrary and perhaps even chauvinistic, like the European colonists who denied souls to native Americans on account of their skin colour.

Emotion is as emotion does

An alternative and less chauvinistic approach would be to define emotion in terms of behaviour rather than of particular brain structures. According to this view, the essence of emotion consists in *behaving* emotionally rather than in the circuitry that mediates that behaviour. Emotion *is* as emotion *does*. By this definition, a computer could be said to have emotions if it behaved in an emotional way. Now the problem becomes one of saying what emotional behaviour consists of, and how it differs from non-emotional behaviour.

In humans and other animals, we tend to call behaviour emotional when we observe certain facial and vocal expressions such as smiling or snarling, and when we see certain physiological changes such as hair standing on end or sweating. Since most computers do not yet possess faces or bodies, they cannot manifest this behaviour. However, in recent years computer scientists have been developing a range of 'animated agent faces', programs that generate images of human-like faces on the computer's visual display unit. These images can be manipulated to form convincing emotional expressions. Others have taken things further by building three-dimensional synthetic heads. Rodney Brooks and colleagues at the Massachusetts Institute of Technology have constructed a robot called 'Kismet' with movable eyelids, eyes, and lips. The range of emotional expressions available to Kismet is limited, but they are convincing enough to generate sympathy among the humans who interact with him. Brooks invites human parents to play with Kismet on a daily basis. When left alone, Kismet looks sad, but when it detects a human face, it smiles, inviting attention. If the carer moves too fast, a look of fear warns that something is wrong. Human parents who play with Kismet cannot help but respond sympathetically to these simple forms of emotional behaviour.

Does Kismet have emotions, then? It certainly exhibits some emotional behaviour, so, if we define emotions in behavioural terms, we must admit that Kismet has some emotional capacity. Kismet does not display the full range of emotional behaviour we observe in humans, but the capacity for emotion is not an all-or-nothing thing. Chimpanzees do not display the full range of human emotions, but they clearly have

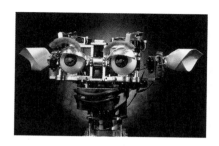

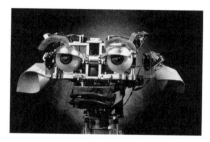

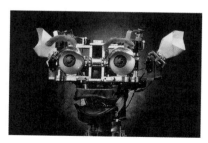

19 Kismet, a robot developed at MIT, has a range of emotional expressions, including happiness, sadness, and surprise.

some emotions. Dogs and cats have less emotional resemblance to us, and those doting pet-owners who ascribe the full range of human emotions to their domestic animals are surely guilty of anthropomorphism, but to deny they had any emotions at all would surely be to commit the opposite, and equally egregious, error of anthropocentrism. There is a whole spectrum of emotional capacities, ranging from the very simple to the very complex. Perhaps Kismet's limited capacity for emotion puts him somewhere near the simple end of the spectrum, but even this is a significant advance over the computers that currently sit on our desks, which by most definitions are devoid of any emotion whatsoever.

As affective computing progresses, we may be able to build machines with more and more complex emotional capacities. Kismet does not yet have a voice, but in the future Brooks plans to give him a vocal system, which might convey auditory signals of emotion. Today's speech synthesizers speak in an unemotional monotone. In the future, computer scientists should be able to make them sound much more human by modulating nonlinguistic aspects of vocalization such as speed, pitch, and volume.

Some progress has already been made in this direction. Janet Cahn has designed a program that can speak in emotional tones. In one experiment, she fed the computer emotionally neutral sentences such as 'I saw your name in the paper', and then instructed it to say the sentence in a way that sounded sad. When human listeners were asked to say what emotion the voice synthesizer was expressing, 91 per cent of them guessed right. The program was not so good at expressing other emotions, but humans are not always successful in conveying their emotions by vocal signals alone either.

Facial expression and vocal intonation are not the only forms of emotional behaviour. We also infer emotions from actions. When, for example, we see an animal stop abruptly in its tracks, turn round, and run away, we infer that it is afraid, even though we may not see the object of its fear. For computers to exhibit this kind of emotional behaviour, they will have to be able to move around. In the jargon of artificial intelligence, they will have to be 'mobots' (mobile robots).

During the autumn of 1999 I went to a lecture at which a variety of real mobots were demonstrated. Some of these mobots were very simple. One, for example, was only the size of a shoe, and all it did was find its way around a piece of the floor without bumping into anything. Sensors allowed it to detect obstacles such as walls and other mobots. Despite the simplicity of this mechanism, the behaviour was quite animal-like.

When an obstacle was detected, the mobot stopped dead in its tracks, turned around, and headed off in the other direction. To all watching, the impression that the mobot was afraid of collisions was irresistible.

Was the mobot really afraid? Or were the spectators, including me, guilty of anthropomorphism? People once asked the same question about animals. Descartes, for example, claimed that animals did not really have feelings like us because they were just complex machines, without a soul. When they screamed in apparent pain, they were just following the dictates of their inner mechanism. Now that we know that the pain mechanism in humans is not much different from that of other animals, the Cartesian distinction between sentient humans and 'machine-like' animals does not make much sense. In the same way, as we come to build machines more and more like us, the question about whether or not the machines have 'real' emotions or just 'fake' ones will become less meaningful. The current resistance to attributing emotions to machines is largely due to the fact that even the most advanced machines today are still very primitive.

Some experts estimate that we will be able to build machines with complex emotions like ours by the year 2050. But is this a good idea? What is the point of building emotional machines? Will not emotions just get in the way of good computing, or, even worse, cause computers to turn against us, as HAL did in *2001*?

Why give computers emotions at all?

Giving computers emotions could be very useful for a whole variety of reasons. For a start, it would be much easier and more enjoyable to interact with an emotional computer than with today's unemotional machines. Imagine if your computer could recognize what emotional state you were in each time you sat down to use it, perhaps by scanning your facial expression. You arrive at work one Monday morning, and the computer detects that you are in a bad mood. Rather than simply asking you for your password, as computers do today, the emotionally aware desktop PC might tell you a joke, or suggest that you read a particularly nice e-mail first. Perhaps it has learnt from previous such mornings that you resent such attempts to cheer you up. In this case, it might ignore you until you had calmed down or had a coffee. It might be much more productive to work with a computer that was emotionally intelligent in this way than with today's dumb machines.

This is not just a flight of fancy. Computers are already capable of recognizing some emotions. Ifran

Essa and Alex Pentland, two American computer scientists, have designed a program that enables a computer to recognize facial expressions of six basic emotions. When volunteers pretended to feel one of these emotions, the computer recognized the emotion correctly 98 per cent of the time. This is even better than the accuracy rate achieved by most humans on the same task. If computers are already better than us at recognizing some emotions, it is surely not long before they will acquire similarly advanced capacities for expressing emotions, and perhaps even for feeling them. In the future, it may be humans who are seen by computers as emotionally illiterate, not vice versa.

What other applications might there be for emotional computers besides providing emotionally intelligent interfaces for desktop PCs? Rosalind Picard, a computer scientist at the MIT Media Laboratory in Boston, has proposed dozens of possible uses, including the following:

- artificial interviewers that train you how to do well in job interviews by giving you feedback on your body language;
- affective voice synthesizers that allow people with speech problems not just to speak, but to speak in genuinely emotional ways;

- frustration monitors that allow manufacturers to evaluate how easy their products are to use;
- wearable computers ('intelligent clothing') that give you feedback on your emotional state, so that you can tell when you are getting stressed and need a break.

All of these applications involve giving computers the ability to recognize what emotions a human is feeling, and to respond appropriately. But what about giving computers the ability to feel emotions themselves? What possible use could this be?

I have already provided part of the answer to this question, when I argued in Chapter Two that Spock could never have evolved. We saw that a creature without emotions could not survive in a dangerous and unpredictable world like ours. Emotions are not luxuries. Still less are they obstacles to intelligent action. They are vital to the survival of any reasonably complex creature.

The same point applies to mobile robots. A robot that is not confined to the safe environment of the laboratory will sooner or later be confronted by dangers such as moving objects or deep holes. If the robot is being directed by a human via remote control, the human can steer the robot around or away from such obstacles. But it is not always desirable to make the robot so

20 Wearable computers are still bulky, but they are becoming lighter and smaller every year. Soon it may be possible for such 'intelligent clothing' to monitor our emotional state.

dependent on a human driver. Nor is it always possible. When the spacecraft Deep Space 1 flew past the asteroid Braille in July 1999, it was too far away from earth for ground control to direct all its movements. The radio waves took too long to travel from earth to the spacecraft, so split-second decisions had to be taken by the spacecraft itself, using its on-board autonomous navigation ('auto-nav') software to plot its own course. It even made its own decisions about when to take photographs.

NASA wants more of this 'hands-off' technology, because it frees up the expensive and overbooked Deep Space Network of large radio antennae for more interesting things than routine tracking of spacecraft. It also allows unmanned spacecraft to handle unpredicted events in real time, without waiting for ground control to tell them what to do. Since most spacecraft like Deep Space 1 usually fly at speeds over 50,000 km per hour, this time saving could be vital.

Auto-nav software is just the beginning. Intelligent machines that can make their own decisions and cope with unpredictability will be useful in many other areas beyond spaceflight. They might be used in bomb disposal, micro-surgery, search-and-rescue missions, and espionage. In all these situations, a robot without the capacity to detect dangers and respond accordingly—

without *fear*, that is—would not last very long. A robot with several potentially conflicting goals, such as avoiding obstacles, refuelling, taking photographs, and returning to earth as fast as possible, will need some kind of internal goal management system. The problem of managing conflicting goals is known by computer scientists as 'the robot's dilemma'. Way back in 1967, Herbert Simon—one of the pioneers of artificial intelligence—argued that robots would need emotions to solve this dilemma.

Simon's argument was simple but clever. There is a limit to the amount of things that any agent can do at any one time, whether it be an animal or a robot. Therefore, if the agent has more than one goal, it must divide its time up wisely, allotting the right amount to each activity in pursuit of each goal. However, unless the environment is completely stable and benign, the agent must also remain alert to external changes that may require a rapid change of activity. Suppose, for example, that a robot has the following two goals: *first* to collect rock samples from an asteroid and analyse them *in situ*, and, *secondly*, to bring these samples safely back to earth. Now imagine that such a robot is sitting happily on the asteroid, conducting some chemical test on the rock it has just picked up, when suddenly a piece of debris comes hurtling towards it. Unless the robot has some kind of 'interruption mechanism', it may succeed in its first goal, but fail dismally in the second.

Simon proposed that emotions were just such interruption mechanisms. He meant this as a definition. In other words, the word 'emotion' is the name we have given to these interruption mechanisms when we have observed them in ourselves and other animals. This is not a neurobiological *or* a behavioural definition of emotion, but a functional one. Functional definitions are like behavioural definitions in that they define mental processes by reference to observable actions, but, unlike full-blooded behaviourists, functionalists do not require that these actions actually take place for the process to be said to occur. It is enough to say that the action would have resulted if certain other mental processes had been in place too. According to Simon's functional definition, emotions are those mental processes that generally work to interrupt activity in rapid response to a sudden environmental change.

The keyword in this definition is *rapid*. Lots of mental processes can interrupt other processes, but not all do so in rapid response to a sudden change in the environment. A mood may build up gradually in response to many small changes before it is sufficiently powerful to interrupt our thoughts. By identifying emotions with *rapid-response* interruption mechanisms,

Simon may have been too narrow. His definition works well for basic emotions, which are typically of rapid onset, but it fares less well for higher cognitive emotions such as love or envy, which may build up more slowly—usually longer than a few seconds, at least. Like many good definitions, Simon's definition of emotion has its value in highlighting one important feature, but it does not cover all cases.

What if machines evolve emotions on their own?

All of the potential applications for emotional machines discussed so far have been resolutely utilitarian. This is all very well, but I think that most emotional machines in the future will be built not for any practical purpose, but purely for entertainment. If you want to envision the future of affective computing, do not think spacecraft and intelligent clothing—think toys and video games.

Many video games already use simple learning algorithms to control non-player characters, such as monsters and baddies. In *Tomb Raider*, for example, the enemies faced by Lara Croft need only a few shots before they cotton on to your shooting style. If you are lying in wait for a dinosaur, it might remain in the shadows, tempting you to come out and take a pot shot so that it can attack you more easily. These are relatively simple programs, but the constant demand for better games means that the software is continually improving. It might well be that the first genuinely emotional computers are games consoles rather than spacecraft.

Other entertainment software with proto-emotional capacities is also available in the form of the virtual pets who live in personal computers. Many kids now keep dogs and cats as screen pets, and more recently a virtual baby has been launched. A program called the Sims lets you design your own people, but they soon take on a life of their own, which can be fascinating to watch. The Sims are eerily human in their range of emotional behaviour. They get angry, become depressed, and even fall in love.

All these creatures are virtual—they live inside your computer, and their only 'body' is a picture on a screen. However, the first computerized creatures with real bodies are also now coming onto the toy market, and they too have proto-emotional capacities. First came little furry robots called 'Furbies', which fall asleep when tired, and make plaintiff cries when neglected for too long. Now there are also robotic dogs and cats that run around your living room without ever making a mess.

As with Kismet, people respond to these artificial life

21 Does the future of emotional computing lie with the entertainment industry? The AIBO Entertainment Robot, produced by Sony, has six emotions: happiness, sadness, anger, surprise, fear, and dislike. Its emotional state changes in accordance with eternal stimuli, and influences its behaviour.

forms with natural sympathy. Their minds are not filled with ponderous doubts about whether these emotions are 'real' or not. They simply enjoy playing with them, as they would with a real kitten or baby. There is even a baby doll with a silicon brain and a latex face that screws up into an expression of distress when it needs feeding.

The gap between science fiction and science fact is closing. Today's computers and robots still have a long way to go before they acquire HAL's emotional reper-toire, but they have already made some progress. In fact, the technology is advancing so quickly that some people are already worried about what will happen when computers and robots become as emotional as we are. Will they turn against their creators, like HAL? In the film *Terminator*, a giant computer called Skynet becomes self-aware and attempts to prevent humans from turning it off by tapping into the military's com-mand system and launching its nuclear missiles. Will affective computing lead ultimately to a battle between humans and machines? If so, who will win? Perhaps in the future robots will no longer be our toys—we may be theirs.

We might be able to avoid this grim fate by program-ming computers to be subservient to us. We might, for example, program them to follow the 'the three laws of robotics', as Isaac Asimov suggested in his short story,

'The Bicentennial Man', which was the inspiration for the film of the same name (see Box below).

However, an important aspect of many emotions is that they are unpredictable. A genuinely emotional robot might decide not to obey these laws, or reinterpret them. And, just as there is a growing respect for animal rights these days, based at least in part on the recognition that non-human animals feel pain and emotions just like human animals, so we might foresee a growing respect for robot rights, based on similar grounds. Just as some people are prepared to use violent means to defend animal rights, so some people might join forces with the oppressed robots to free them from their slavery.

The three laws of robotics

1. A robot may not injure a human being or, through inaction, allow a human being to come to harm.
2. A robot must obey the orders given it by human beings except where such orders would conflict with the First Law.
3. A robot must protect its own existence as long as such protection does not conflict with the First or Second Law.

Source: Isaac Asimov, 'The Bicentennial Man'

Many people might think that computers will always be predictable, since all they ever do is follow a program. The same idea leads people to reject the idea that computers might one day come to have emotions. Even if we design clever software that allows a computer to mimic emotional behaviour, these will not be true emotions, because they will just be following instructions. The computer would not be unpredictable, as genuinely emotional creatures are.

What, then, would these people say of computers that evolve their own programs? Such machines might come to have true emotions of their own, not designed by any human. A relatively recent branch of computer science, known as artificial life, experiments with just such self-evolving software. Instead of writing the program themselves, computer scientists working in artificial life generate random sequences of instructions, and allow these mini-programs (called genetic algorithms) to compete with each other for space on the computer's hard disk. The programs that perform better than others in the task at hand are allowed to make copies of themselves and occupy more memory space, while those that perform badly are erased. The copying process, however, is deliberately made imperfect, so that the occasional error creeps in. This provides for the generation of mutant programs, some of which are even better at performing the chosen task than their parents and so come to dominate the hard disk. If this process is repeated for many generations, the beneficial mutations accumulate, leading to exceptionally effective programs that no human could have designed by normal methods.

It will not have escaped your notice that artificial life is remarkably like evolution by natural selection. In fact, it *is* evolution by natural selection. All the ingredients are there: heredity (they make copies of themselves), mutation (the copies are not perfect), and differential replication (some programs make more copies of themselves than others). The technical term for these self-evolving programs—'genetic algorithms'—makes clear the parallel with DNA-based evolution. The fact that the protagonists are sequences of code on a hard disk rather than sequences of nucleotides on a chromosome does not disqualify artificial life from evolution. Just as it would be parochial to deny that computers could not have emotions because they lack organic brains, so it would be equally parochial to deny that they could evolve simply because they lack DNA. The essence of all biological processes, from emotion and evolution to life itself, lies not in the materials of which they are composed but in how those materials behave. So long as programs can make copies of themselves, some of which are not perfect, and so long as the number of copies made depends on some property of the program itself, the programs can truly be said to evolve by natural selection.

One of the most famous experiments in artificial life involved the creation of a virtual world known as *Tierra*. Designed by the computer scientist Thomas Ray, *Tierra* was initially populated with copies of a single program. As just described, this program had the ability to make copies of itself; it was a 'genetic algorithm'. But the copies were not always perfect, so, as time went on, *Tierra* became filled with an increasingly diverse population of digital organisms. As Ray observed the evolution of his virtual biosphere, he was fascinated to see the emergence of unforeseen life forms, complete with virtual viruses and hosts who developed artificial immune systems to defend themselves. These artificial life forms did not get as far as acquiring emotions, but it is not hard to see how they could come to evolve such capacities, if they were given enough time. Given the random element in the design process, such artificial emotions could be genuinely unpredictable.

The techniques of artificial life may be enough to persuade those who reject the possibility of emotional machines on the grounds that true emotions are unpredictable. Such techniques, however, will probably not be enough to meet the last and most pressing objection to the idea of affective computers. This is the contention that computers will never have true emotions because they will never be conscious. According to this view, computers might come to exhibit emotional *behaviour*, but they will never have that subjective *feeling* that constitutes the essence of true emotion.

As already noted, many people seem to regard feelings as the essence of emotion, but this is not the view taken by most contemporary scientists and philosophers who study emotion. From the viewpoint of modern science, it would be as foolish to deny that a computer could have emotions just because it lacked conscious feelings as to deny that a paralysed person could have emotions simply because he could not make the relevant facial expressions.

Furthermore, the claim that computers could never become conscious is just an intuition. Some rather specious arguments have been put forward to support this intuition, but these thought experiments, involving Chinese rooms and zombies, are even more far-fetched than the idea they oppose (see Box below). The truth is that, at the beginning of the twenty-first century, no one really has much of an idea about what consciousness really is. Given the lack of good ideas about consciousness, and the lack of agreement about how to investigate

Will computers ever become conscious?

Some researchers in artificial intelligence think that machines will become conscious within the next hundred years. Some philosophers think this is ridiculous. They claim that machines could *never* become conscious, and they have devised some curious thought-experiments to support this claim.

In what has now become a classic paper in the philosophy of mind, John Searle proposed the idea of the 'Chinese room'. A man sits in a room into which are fed a series of Chinese inscriptions. He is armed with a set of rules about how to respond to these inscriptions, which he duly carries out. The people outside the room might think that the man knows Chinese, but it is clear to us that he doesn't. He is only following rules. Searle thinks computers will always be like this. They can only follow rules, but never really 'know' anything. By extension, Searle argues that computers could never become conscious.

Another philosopher, David Chalmers, has argued that consciousness is not something that could ever be demonstrated by behaviour alone. He asks us to imagine a zombie, by which he means a being like us in every external way but without consciousness. If such a being were possible, it would show that we cannot definitely attribute consciousness to a computer no matter how conscious it *seems*.

The problem with these thought-experiments is that, to borrow a phrase, there is too much thought and not enough experiment. Rather than trying to decide whether or not computers can become conscious on the basis of far-fetched stories about other things that we are even less sure about, like Chinese rooms and zombies, we would be better off proceeding more experimentally. In short, the only way we will really know whether or not machines can be conscious is by trying to build a conscious machine.

it, all objections against emotional computing based on the supposed impossibility of conscious machines must be taken with a pinch of salt.

One of the few good ideas about consciousness that has gained some measure of agreement is that subjective feelings depend very much on the kind of body you have. This might mean that the digital organisms in *Tierra* could never become conscious, as they are merely virtual. They exist only as sequences of code on a computer's hard disk. More recently, however, computer scientists have begun to extend the techniques of artificial life to computers with real bodies. This fledgling discipline is known as evolutionary robotics. As with artificial life, the idea is to let the program that controls the robot evolve by itself, rather than getting humans to design it. Even if the Tierran organisms could not become conscious, such embodied programs might be able to.

If emotions are vital to the survival of any half-intelligent creature, as I argued in Chapter Two, we should expect these complex robots to evolve their own emotions just as the higher animals have done. Left to their own devices, such robots might come to evolve emotions very different from our own. The emotions that a creature needs to survive depend very much on the creature's lifestyle and habitat. If the creature lives a largely solitary existence, it will not need social emotions such as guilt and jealousy. If there are no predators to prey on it, it may not need the capacity to feel afraid. Depending on how different the lifestyle and habitat of robots are from our own, they may come to evolve rather alien kinds of emotion.

Even if robot emotions turn out to be superficially identical to human emotions, they may *feel* very different to the robots themselves. If there really is a close link between consciousness and the details of the body, the subjective feel of our emotions may be determined by the precise details of our physiology. Emotional robots with plastic or metal bodies would then almost certainly have rather different inner sensations from emotional humans with fleshy bodies. Given that

22 Love between man and robot? Or between two robots? In this scene from the film *Blade Runner*, Deckard (played by Harrison Ford) kisses Rachael (played by Sean Young). Rachael is a robot; perhaps Deckard is too.

sympathy involves taking on the emotions of another and feeling them as if they were one's own, the different physiologies of robots and humans might make it very hard for us to sympathize with them, even if they displayed very human-like behaviour. More dangerously, perhaps, it might be equally difficult for robots to sympathize with us. Once again, the nightmare scenario of a war between humans and robots seems to loom.

Perhaps our fears of a future battle for supremacy between man and machine are misplaced. Complex robots that evolve their own emotions might come to be our friends rather than our enemies. *Bicentennial Man* and *Blade Runner* both show humans and robots falling in love with each other.

Such images of friendly robots are even more common in Japan than in the West. The emotional machines that will almost certainly exist in the not too far distant future may even turn out to be our salvation, guiding us out of our hostility towards them by educating us to emulate their own, much more refined sensibility.

Afterword

The heart has its reasons

'The heart has its reasons,' wrote Blaise Pascal, 'of which reason knows nothing.' When people speak of cognition and emotion, or (in more traditional vocabulary) of reason and the passions, they are usually referring to two distinct mental faculties. One of them is cool and calm and collected, and works towards its conclusions slowly by means of explicit logical rules. The other is hot and colourful, and jumps to conclusions by consulting gut feelings. However, just because the heart works independently of *reason* does not mean it lacks *reasons*. On the contrary, as I have tried to show in this book, the things that emotions do, from making us flee from danger and prompting us to court attractive people, to concentrating our minds and influencing our judgements, all have their reasons, and sometimes these reasons are very good ones. Not only are there passions within reason, but there are reasons within passion.

Take the mere-exposure effect, for example. In Chapter Four, I explained how we tend to prefer things we have seen before, simply because they are familiar. Human beings are creatures of habit, and 'Better the devil you know' seems to be our motto. This might seem a silly way to behave, but in fact it serves us pretty well. A recent study by the German psychologist Gerd Gigerenzer, Dan Goldstein, and colleagues at the Centre for Adaptive Behaviour and Cognition in Berlin showed that, in many situations when people have to make a choice between several alternatives, those who simply choose the familiar option do better than those who make their minds up on the basis of more sophisticated reasoning. Even in factual tests, people who rely on this 'recognition heuristic' often do better. For example, when Gigerenzer and Goldstein asked Americans to decide which of two German cities was larger, those who simply guessed by choosing the city whose name they recognized scored more highly than those who tried to work it out on the basis of explicit knowledge.

Another way in which emotions and moods affect judgement is the well-known relationship between good mood and overconfidence. People in a good mood regularly overestimate their chances of succeeding at a given activity, while those in a bad mood tend to be more accurate in their predictions (a phenomenon known as 'depressive realism'). You might think that those in a bad mood would be better off, since, other things being equal, accurate predictions are better than inaccurate ones. The problem is that other things are *not* equal. If your chances of succeeding are quite low, and you are in a bad mood, then your accurate estimation of these chances may put you off even trying. If, however, you are in a good mood, your inflated hopes of success may encourage you to have a go, and you may end up being one of the lucky ones. If the costs of wasted effort are low, and the rewards for success are high, then it will pay to be over-optimistic. Any attempt on our part to bring our expectations more into line with the objective chances of success may drive those levels down further still. And, even when overconfidence does not actually increase your chances of success, it may bring other benefits of a more social nature, such as attracting partners or inspiring trust.

Such examples may seem paradoxical. On one level, being in a good mood seems to make people *less* rational by leading them to have higher expectations of success than the objective facts justify. On another level, however, being overconfident can be more rational than being realistic, since some prizes only go to the bold. It seems that emotions can sometimes exhibit a kind of super-rationality that saves pure reason from itself.

This is not true of emotions all the time. If it were, the negative view of emotion would never have got off the ground, let alone achieved the influence it has achieved. The fact that emotions have got such a bad press in the writings of many Western thinkers is testimony to the fact that they do not always trump reason for good. Sometimes their effects on our reasoning are positively harmful. The mere-exposure effect may lead us to spend our money on familiar brand names rather than on cheaper products that are just as good but manufactured by lesser-known companies. The effects of mood on judgement mean that we may be taken in by a con artist simply because his friendly face produces a good gut feeling that blinds us to the holes in his arguments. And so on.

The positive view of emotion, which I have defended in this book, does not deny that emotions sometimes affect our reasoning to our detriment. It simply claims that these occasions are outnumbered and outweighed by the occasions on which emotions affect our reasoning for the better. On balance, a creature who lacked emotions would not just be less *intelligent* than we are; it would be less *rational* too.

This suggests that we should take a rather different

view of rationality than that proposed by logicians and economists. Economists define rationality in a rather technical way, as the maximization of one's expected utility. Roughly speaking, this means that a rational person is one who, given a certain set of preferences, will act in such a way as to satisfy as many of those preferences as possible. This is all well and good as far as it goes, but it says nothing about where those preferences come from, nor whether it is rational to have some preferences rather than others. Indeed, the last question is, strictly speaking, meaningless for economists, since they define rationality in terms of satisfying preferences. There may be irrational *consumers* and irrational *purchases* (that is, those that could not be the result of a 'consistent' set of preferences), but there is no such thing, in economics, as an irrational *preference* (or a rational one, for that matter; preferences just *are*).

This seems crazy to me. It seems perfectly sensible to ask whether or not it is rational to have a certain preference. For example, I think that it is reasonable to want to be liked by a few friends but unreasonable to want to be adored by everyone in the world. If economists regard such statements as nonsense, it is because *they* are out of step with the rest of the world, not because the rest of the world is out of step with *them*. The heart has its reasons too, but these reasons are not the reasons of means–ends *reasoning*; emotions are not just about how to achieve a given end, but also about what ends to pursue in the first place. If we want a name for this enlarged notion of rationality, we might follow Gigerenzer in calling it 'ecological rationality'. Another term might be 'evolutionary rationality', since our preferences are heavily influenced by our biological inheritance. If the heart has its reasons, this is because natural selection designed our emotions just as it designed our other mental faculties: to help us survive and reproduce as best we could in a dangerous and exciting world.

Further reading

There has been an avalanche of good books on emotion in recent years, so readers wishing to know more are spoilt for choice. Here I recommend some general introductions that cover the subject in more detail than I do in this book, and provide more specific ideas for further reading on the topics discussed in each chapter. Wherever possible, I have recommended books rather than journal articles, as books are easier for most people to get hold of. This section is for the general reader; I have provided information about more technical works for the academic reader in the section entitled 'Source Material'.

General Introductions to the Study of Emotion

For a more comprehensive and more academic, but nonetheless extremely readable, introduction to the study of emotion, you could not do better than to read Keith Oatley and Jennifer M. Jenkins, *Understanding Emotions* (Oxford: Blackwell, 1996). For a more philosophical approach, try Paul Griffiths, *What Emotions Really Are: The Problem of Psychological Categories* (Chicago: University of Chicago Press, 1997), Aaron Ben-Ze'ev, *The Subtlety of Emotions* (Cambridge, Mass: MIT Press, 2000), and Peter Goldie, *The Emotions: A Philosophical Exploration* (Oxford: Oxford University Press, 2000). Two very accessible accounts of the neuroscience of emotion are Joseph LeDoux, *The Emotional Brain* (London: Weidenfeld & Nicolson, 1998), and Antonio Damasio, *Descartes' Error: Emotion, Reason and the Human Brain* (New York:

Putnam, 1994; London: Macmillan, 1995). For a view from cognitive science and AI, my next book, *Rethinking Emotion*, takes some of the arguments in this book a little further (Cambridge, Mass.: MIT Press, forthcoming). Finally, I warmly recommend Adam Smith, *The Theory of Moral Sentiments*; a cheap paperback edition is published by the Liberty Fund (Indianapolis, 1984). Originally published in 1759, Smith's first book still remains a wonderfully acute study of emotion. It also makes clear that Smith did not believe humans to be essentially selfish creatures, as some have surmised on reading his other book, *An Inquiry into the Nature and Causes of the Wealth of Nations* (1776).

Emotions and Cultural Variation

For a defence of the cultural theory of emotion, see Rom Harré (ed.), *The Social Construction of Emotion* (Oxford: Blackwell, 1986). The essay by Heelas in this volume is a good source of information about culturally specific emotions; Heelas takes the reader on what he calls a 'Cook's tour' of emotions in different cultures.

C. S. Lewis proposes his crazy thesis that romantic love was invented by medieval European poets in *The Allegory of Love: A Study in Medieval Tradition* (Oxford: Oxford University Press, 1936). A wonderful account of love in the stone age is provided by Geoffrey Miller in chapter 6 of his book *The Mating Mind* (London: Heinemann, 2000).

Emotions and Evolution

An excellent new edition of Darwin's 1872 work on *The Expression of Emotions in Man and Animals*, with notes by Paul Ekman, has recently been published by Weidenfeld & Nicolson (1998). A summary of more recent evolutionary accounts of emotion is provided by Randolph Nesse in 'Evolutionary Explanations of Emotions', *Human Nature*, 1 (1990), 261–89.

Robert Frank argues persuasively for his innovative theory of higher cognitive emotions in *Passions within Reason: The Strategic Role of the Emotions*, in which he also describes the experiment about estimating the trustworthiness of strangers (New York and London: Norton, 1988). Daniel Goleman describes work on emotional intelligence in *Emotional Intelligence* (New York: Bantam Books, 1995).

Moods and happiness

The World Database of Happiness can be accessed online at http://www.eur.nl/fsw/research/happiness. Lewis Wolpert presents a good overall view of depression in *Malignant Sadness: The Anatomy of Depression* (London: Faber and Faber, 1999).

Effects of Emotion on Cognition

An excellent overview of the effects of emotion on cognitive processes is provided by Keith Oatley and Jennifer Jenkins in chapter 9 of their book *Understanding Emotions* (Oxford: Blackwell, 1996), on which I have drawn heavily in writing Chapter Four. For a historical perspective, see the book on rhetoric by Aristotle, Plato's *Gorgias*, and volume 6 of the *Institutio Oratoria* by Quintillian. The stoics had surprisingly modern things to say about this topic, as Richard Sorabji argues in *Emotion and Peace of Mind: From Stoic Agitation to Christian Temptation* (Oxford: Oxford University Press, 2000).

Most of the material referred to in Chapter Four takes the form of articles published in academic journals. For those without access to such journals, a good sourcebook covering many of the same issues is J. P. Forgas (ed.), *Emotion and Social Judgements* (Oxford: Pergamon, 1991).

Emotions and Computers
A comprehensive overview of theoretical and technical research in how to give computers emotions is provided by Rosalind Picard, *Affective Computing* (Cambridge, Mass., and London: MIT Press, 1997). For a more general introduction to artificial intelligence, see John Haugeland, *Artificial Intelligence: The Very Idea* (Cambridge, Mass., and London: MIT Press, 1985). Andy Clark, *Being There: Putting Brain, Body and World Together Again* (Cambridge, Mass., and London: MIT Press, 1997), provides an excellent overview of recent work in robotics from a philosophical perspective. The connection between consciousness, feelings, and physiology is explored by Nicholas Humphrey in *A History of the Mind* (New York: Copernicus, 1992).

Last but not least, I recommend Isaac Asimov's science-fiction story, 'The Bicentennial Man', which can be found in *The Bicentennial Man and Other Stories* (New York: Doubleday, 1976). In this story Asimov manages to explore many of the moral dilemmas of giving computers emotions more effectively than any non-fiction account.

Source material

For students and academic readers, here are some of the original sources I have worked from.

Chapter 1

Paul Ekman outlines his theory of basic emotions and sets out the evidence in 'An Argument for Basic Emotions', *Cognition and Emotion*, 6 (1992), 169–200. The Gururumba emotion of 'being a wild pig' is discussed by P. L. Newman in ' "Wild Man" Behaviour in a New Guinea Highlands Community', *American Anthropologist*, 66 (1964), 1–19. The idea that such culturally specific emotions serve important social functions is due to the psychologist James Averill, who explains this view in detail in 'A Constructivist View of Emotion', a chapter in R. Plutchik and H. Kellerman (eds.), *Emotion: Theory, Research and Experience*, i, *Theories of Emotion*, (New York: Academic Press, 1980). The tendency for ideas about the human mind to become self-fulfilling prophecies is discussed by Ian Hacking in his fascinating book, *Rewriting the Soul: Multiple Personality and the Sciences of Memory* (Princeton: Princeton University Press, 1995).

Chapter 2

The experimental work on fear learning in monkeys is reported by S. Mineka and M. Cook, 'Mechanisms Involved in the Observational Conditioning of Fear', *Journal of Experimental Psychology: General*, 122 (1993) 23–38. Haleh Samiei gives a good summary of evolutionary explanations of crying in 'Why we Weep', *Washington Post*, 12 January 2000, p. H06. William Frey argues that crying makes us feel better by getting rid of stress hormones in *Crying: The Mystery of Tears* (Minneapolis: Winston Press, 1985). Randolph Cornelius puts forward the opposing view, that it is the social support we receive after crying that makes us feel better, in *The Science of Emotion* (Upper Saddle River, NJ: Prentice Hall, 1995). The neuroanatomy of emotion in humans and other animals is clearly explained by Joseph LeDoux in *The Emotional Brain* (London: Weidenfeld & Nicolson, 1998). LeDoux is critical of Paul MacLean's concept of the limbic system, but it is still worth having a look at MacLean's classic treatise, *A Triune Concept of the Brain and Behaviour* (Toronto: University of Toronto Press, 1973).

An excellent summary of Robert Frank's theory is provided by Steven Pinker in chapter 6 of *How the Mind Works* (New York: Norton, 1997; Harmondsworth: Penguin: 1998). The parable of the protesters, and the quote from Douglas Yates, are both taken from this chapter. The concept of emotional intelligence was first put forward by Peter Salovey and John Mayer in 'Emotional Intelligence', *Imagination, Cognition and Personality*, 9 (1990), 185–211. For further information about psychopathy and the development of moral reasoning see James Blair, 'A Cognitive Developmental Approach to Morality: Investigating the Psychopath', in Simon Baron-Cohen (ed.), *The Maladapted Mind: Classic Readings in Evolutionary Psychopathology* (Hove: Psychology Press, 1997).

Chapter 3
A number of essays reviewing the latest research in the

psychology of happiness are published in the January 2000 edition of *American Psychologist*. Two studies that throw doubt on Adam Smith's views on the perils of good fortune are H. Roy Kaplan, 'Lottery Winners: The Myth and Reality', *Journal of Gambling Behaviour*, 3 (1987), 168–78, and Mark Abrahamson, 'Sudden Wealth, Gratification and Attainment: Durkheim's Anomie of Affluence Reconsidered', *American Sociological Review*, 45 (1980), 49–57. A more anecdotal account of lottery jackpot winners that also goes along with the 'winning doesn't make you unhappy' theory is Hunter Davies, *Living on the Lottery* (London: Little, Brown, 1996).

Aaron Beck discusses cognitive therapy in *Cognitive Therapy and the Emotional Disorders* (New York: Meridian, 1976). Geoffrey Miller argues for the idea that jokes and stories please us because they provide information about the narrator's intelligence in chapter 10 of *The Mating Mind* (London: Heinemann, 2000). For a discussion of the hydraulic theory of emotion and the 'venting myth' of emotional expression, see Eileen Kennedy-Moore and Jeanne C. Watson, *Expressing Emotion: Myths, Realities and Therapeutic Strategies* (New York and London: Guildford Press, 1999). Sigmund Freud and Josef Breuer first presented their 'talking cure' in the still highly readable *Studies on Hysteria,* first published in 1895; a paperback version is published as volume 3 in The Pelican Freud Library (Harmondsworth: Penguin, 1974). Martha Nussbaum explores what Aristotle really meant by the term 'catharsis' in *The Fragility of Goodness: Luck and Ethics in Greek Tragedy and Philosophy* (Cambridge: Cambridge University Press, 1986). The idea that the theatre is ideal for catharsis because it allows us to experience emotions at 'a best aesthetic distance' is discussed by Thomas Scheff in *Catharsis in Healing, Ritual and*

Drama (Berkeley and Los Angeles: University of California Press, 1979). The negative effects of debriefing are exposed by Jo Rick and Rob Briner in their paper 'Trauma Management vs. Stress Debriefing: What should Responsible Organisations do?', which can be downloaded from the web by visiting http://www.employment-studies.co.uk and following the links to press releases and articles.

Nicholas Humphrey describes his experiments on the effects of colour in chapter 8 of *A History of the Mind* (New York: Copernicus, 1992); there is also some relevant information in chapter 6. The emotional effects of *Eine kleine Nachtmusik* are described by P. M. Niedenthal and M. B. Setterlund in 'Emotion Congruence in Perception', *Personality and Social Psychology Bulletin*, 20 (1994), 401–11. Aniruddh Patel and Evan Balaban present intriguing data about the neural response to melody in their article 'Temporal Patterns of Human Cortical Activity Reflect Tone Sequence Structure', *Nature*, 404 (2 Mar. 2000), 80–4. The neurochemistry of mood, and the effects of Prozac, are described by David Healy in his wonderfully informative book, *The Antidepressant Era* (Cambridge, Mass., and London: Harvard University Press, 1997). The venerable history of drug use for therapeutic, recreational, and ritual purposes is detailed in J. Goodman and P. Sherratt (eds.), *Consuming Habits: Drugs in History and Anthropology* (London: Routledge, 1995).

William James first put forward his novel theory of emotion in his classic 1884 essay, 'What is an Emotion?', which is reprinted in various anthologies, such as Magda Arnold (ed.), *The Nature of Emotion* (Harmondsworth: Penguin, 1968). Paul Ekman and Wallace Friesen describe their experiments on the emotional effects of adopting certain facial expressions in their paper 'Autonomic

Nervous System Activity Distinguishes among Emotions', by Ekman, Levenson, *et. al.,* in *Science,* 221 (1983), 1208–10.

Chapter 4

The original Stroop test is explained by J. R. Stroop himself in 'Studies of Interference in Serial Verbal Reactions', *Journal of Experimental Psychology,* 18 (1935), 643–62. The results of various experiments based on the emotional Stroop test are summarized by A. Matthews in 'Biases in Emotional Processing', *Psychologist,* 6 (1993), 493–9. The experiment on the effects of emotion on visual memory is reported by S. A. Christianson and E. Loftus in 'Remembering Emotional Events: The Fate of Detailed Informa- tion', *Cognition and Emotion,* 5 (1991), 81–108. Gordon Bower discusses a number of his own experiments on mood-congruent recall in 'Mood and Memory', *American Psychologist,* 36 (1981), 129–48. The experiment on the effects of mood on interviewer's judgements is reported by R. A. Baron in 'Interviewer's Mood and Reaction to Job Applicants', *Journal of Applied Social Psychology,* 17 (1987), 911–26.

The wonderful experiment about the bonding effects of anxiety is discussed by D. G. Dutton and A. P. Aron in 'Some Evidence for Heightened Sexual Attraction under Conditions of High Anxiety', *Journal of Personality and Social Psychology,* 30 (1974), 510–17. Diane Mackie and Leila Worth explain their experiments on the effects of mood on susceptibility to weak arguments in 'Processing Deficits and the Mediation of Positive Affect in Persuasion', *Journal of Personality and Social Psychology,* 57 (1989), 27–40. Antonio Damasio tells the story of his hyper- rational patient on page 193 of *Descartes' Error: Emotion, Reason and the Human Brain* (London: Picador, 1995). Robert Frank's experiment on the accuracy of our sense of trust is discussed in chapter 7 of his book *Passions within Reason: The Strategic Role of the Emotions* (New York and London: Norton, 1988). Robert Zajonc recounts his research on the mere-exposure effect in 'Feeling and Thinking: Preferences Need no Inferences', *American Psychologist*, 35 (1980), 151–75.

Chapter 5

My argument against defining emotions in neurobiological terms is adapted from Hilary Putnam's famous argument against the identity theory of mind, which he put forward in a 1960 paper entitled 'Psychological Predicates'. This paper is republished as 'The Nature of Mental States', in *Mind and Cognition: An Anthology*, 2nd edn. edited by William G. Lycan (Oxford: Blackwell, 1999), 27–34. Janet Cahn discusses her emotional speech program in 'The Generation of Affect in Synthesized Speech', *Journal of the American Voice I/O Society*, 8 (1990), 1–19. Ifran Essa and Alex Pentland describe their work on computer recognition of facial affect in 'Coding, Analysis, Interpretation and Recognition of Facial Expressions', *IEEE Transactions on Pattern Analysis and Machine Intelligence*, 19 (1997), 757–63.

Herbert Simon's prophetic remarks about the need to give computers and robots some kind of emotional system can be found in his article 'Motivational and Emotional Controls of Cognition', *Psychological Review*, 74 (1967), 29–39. A good selection of papers about artificial life is collected together in Margaret Boden (ed.), *The Philosophy of Artificial Life* (Oxford: Oxford University Press, 1996). Among the articles in this volume is the 1992 paper by Thomas Ray, 'An Approach to the Synthesis of Life', in which he describes his *Tierra* program.

Afterword

Ecological rationality and the 'recognition heuristic' are discussed in Gerd Gigerenzer, Peter M. Todd, and the ABC Research Group, *Simple Heuristics that Make us Smart* (Oxford: Oxford University Press, 1999).

Illustrations

1. Facial expressions of basic emotions. Fig. 3.2 of P. Ekman and W. V. Friesen: *Unmasking the Face: A Guide to Recognizing Emotions from Facial Expressions.* Englewood Cliffs, N. J./ Prentice-Hall, 1975.
   Paul Ekman and Wallace V. Freisen

2. Two self-portrait etchings by Rembrandt, 1630. Surprise and anger/contempt.
   Photo: AKG London

3. Four video stills of a New Guinea Highlander with different facial expressions, taken by Dr Paul Ekman.
   Paul Ekman

4. *Romeo and Juliet*, 1884, by Sir Frank Dicksee (1853–1928).
   Southampton City Art Gallery, Hampshire, UK/Bridgeman Art Library

5. Leonard Nimoy as Mr Spock in *Star Trek II: The Wrath of Khan*, 1982.
   Ronald Grant Archive/Paramount Pictures

6. 'You're so emotional. . .' (cartoon by Jacky Fleming).
   © Jacky Fleming, from *Hello Boys*, Penguin 1996

7. The low and the high roads of the amygdala.
   Joseph le Doux: *The Emotional Brain*, 1998. Weidenfeld & Nicholson Ltd., London.

8. Cat, savage and prepared to fight. Wood engraving by Thomas William Wood (*fl.* 1855–1872).
   From 1872 edition of Darwin's *The Expression of the Emotions*.

9. Location of the hippocampus and amygdala and surrounding cortical areas.

   J. H. Martin: *Neuroanatomy: Text and Atlas*, Elsevier, 1989. © 1989 Appleton and Lange. By permission of the McGraw-Hill companies

10. *Jealousy and Flirtation*, by Haynes King (1831–1904).

    Victoria and Albert Museum, Londond/Bridgeman Art Library

11. 'It could be you', British National Lottery poster, with hand coming out of sky.

    The National Lottery/Camelot Group

12. Mature man wearing headphones, eyes closed.

    © Colin Hawkins/Stone

13. The priestess Ihat sniffing a lotus flower, Egyptian relief carving, *c.* 2494–2345 BC

    Egyptian Museum, Cairo/Werner Forman Archive

14. People dancing at a rave.

    © Eve Brownlow/Sally & Richard Greenhill

15. The three versions of the critical eighth slide in the sequence used by Christianson and Loftus.

    S. A. Christianson and E. Loftus, 1991, 'Remembering Emotional Events: The Fate Of Detailed Information', *Cognition and Emotion*, 5, 81–108

16. Graph of results from Mackie and Worth experiment.

    Drawing by the author based on numerical table in Mackie and Worth, 1989, p. 34.

17. Hitler addresses two million people on May Day, 1934.

    © Hulton Getty

18. Hal from *2001: A Space Odyssey*, 1968.

    Ronald Grant Archive/Warner Brothers

19. Kismet, robot developed at MIT, which imitates a range of 'human' emotions. Here sadness, happiness, and surprise.
Peter Menzel/Science Photo Library

20. Mobile Assistant IV fi, portable voice-operated computer by US firm Xybernaut.
Xybernaut Corporation, USA

21. The AIBO Entertainment Robot, produced by Sony.
'AIBO' Entertainment Robot ERS-111 © Copyright Sony Corporation, 1999

22. Harrison Ford kissing Sean Young, from *Blade Runner*, 1982.
Ronald Grant Archive/Warner Brothers

Index